OBAMA
CONFIDENTIAL

Strange, Odd, and Bizarre
Letters to the 44th President

OBAMA

CONFIDENTIAL

STRANGE, ODD, AND BIZARRE
LETTERS TO THE 44TH PRESIDENT

BY

MARC BERLIN

BB
BOOKS

A DIVISION OF BSF LLC

Published by BB Books, a Division of BSF LLC.

© 2013 by Marc Berlin

ISBN: 978-0-9859624-1-8

For more information, visit www.obamaconfidential.com.

Printed in the United States of America.
Book design by MonkeyPAWcreative.

To the Voters of Ohio

DISCLAIMER

"Obama Confidential: Strange, Odd, and Bizarre Letters
to the 44th President" is a work of satire by Marc Berlin, and
is not intended maliciously. The author has invented all names
and situations in its stories. Any use of real names of any actual
persons, living or dead, is entirely accidental and coincidental.
In cases where public figures are being satirized, the facts
may be totally invented for the sake of parody,
humor, or amusement.

Also by Marc Berlin

That Cloud Looks Like Jesus
The Skeptic's Handbook

TABLE OF CONTENTS

Mail bins in the
White House basement.

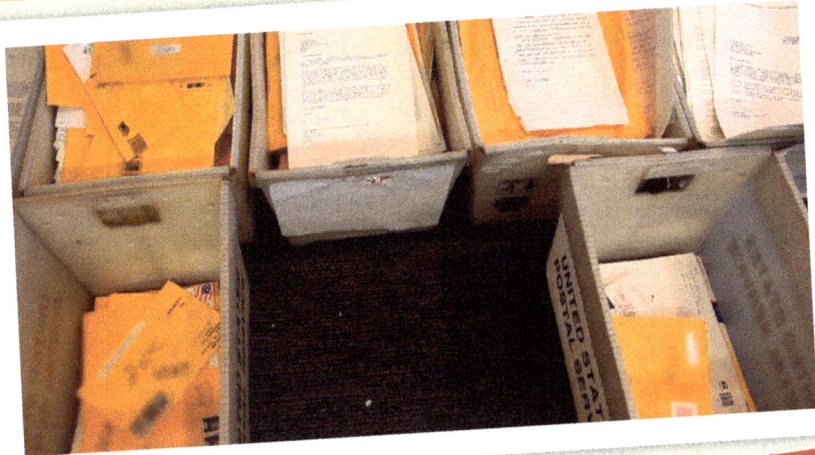

Almost none of these letters
will ever be read.

ABERCROMBIE WAX CO.

September 15, 2012

Dear President Obama:

On behalf of all the employees and senior staff here at The Abercrombie Wax Company, Inc., I would like to sincerely thank you for your recent visit to our plant in Elyria.

I can assure you that all of us were not only excited by your 12-minute visit, but also filled with pride as you quickly toured the plant floor, then listened patiently to each of our little "worker bees" as they explained what was required to get the product out to our customers across the Buckeye State, and beyond.

Also, I want to apologize for the negative comments you might have heard while delivering your short "pep-talk" just before noon. They did NOT represent the cross section of our workers, and the only explanation I can find is that some in the crowd were hungry as they had not eaten lunch yet and they took it out on you. Several of those responsible have been reprimanded, and one was later terminated for complaining to a co-worker about your being here.

I'm sad to report, Mr. President, that just after you left, Bill Czezswezsciski, (the operator of the forklift you rode on for a few seconds in shipping), was slightly injured when he fell into a vat of soybean wax. We think Bill was so darn excited by your visit that he put his lift into reverse instead of forward by mistake. Fortunately, several of our staff acted quickly and were able to pull him out of the vat before anything serious could happen. Still, it was pretty scary.

If you're ever in Elyria again, or even Lakewood which is just north of us, please have the SS guys call me on my private number and we'll be happy to arrange another tour. Good luck in your second term !

Yours truly,

Clint Roswell

Clint Roswell, Jr.
Sr. V.P. for Public Affairs
Abercrombie Wax Co.
1-440-555-4443 Ext. 23

THE WHITE HOUSE

WASHINGTON

October 20, 2012

Dear Clint:

    Thanks for your kind letter. I'll always remember my visit to Abercrombie Wax. I never fully appreciated what actually goes into making wax, but when I got home a few days later and told Sasha and Malia, they said they wanted to visit you guys, too.

    Ohio, the 'Mother of Presidents' and 'Birthplace of Aviation', is a great state, populated by patriotic, hard-working Americans. Please stay in touch.

Sincerely,

Barack Obama

January 16, 2012

Dear Mr. President,

    My name is Al Kayda.   I am currently a resident of Milwaukee Wisconsin, where I own a small dry cleaning business. I am writing to you today out of desperation.

    Because of my name, since September 11, 2001 I have been subjected to various forms of punishment -- for a crime I never committed !

    For example, when customers enter my shop and find out my name, they often turn and walk out. When I talk to people on the phone, they very often immediately hang up. If I go to a party, once they discover my name people refuse to talk to me.

    All this has been barely tolerable. But the straw that broke the camel's back was when the IRS started to audit me. Every year since 2001 an IRS agent has visited my home for an in-depth week-long audit even though my tax returns are professionally prepared by a CPA with over twenty years of experience.

    Mr. President, to make matters even worse, if that's possible, several members of my immediate family who haven't changed their names yet have been subjected not only to taunts and verbal threats, but to actual physical harm just outside their homes in the Milwaukee area and in Madison. Luckily, no

serious injuries have occurred yet, but it's
only a matter of time.

I complained to the local authorities, as
well as to the regional office of the FBI, but
no one ever called me back or followed up.

Sir, I am pleading with you now: if
there's anything, anything at all you could do
to help me and my family, I would be eternally
grateful. I am a hard-working American who has
up to now played by all the rules.
Unfortunately, at least for me, the rules
aren't working.

Sincerely,

Albert G. Kayda

THE WHITE HOUSE

WASHINGTON

September 30, 2012

Dear Mr. Kayda,

Thank you for your letter regarding the problems you're having with
your name. Wisconsin, the Badger State, is a truly beautiful place. Even
though it's not the Mother of Presidents like Ohio, it's still "America's
Dairyland" and makes great cheese. I'm gratified you're playing by the rules,
as all Americans should. Keep up the good work.

Sincerely,

Barack Obama

October 17, 2012

Greetings Mr. President,

My name is Zen Aprobeen-5. I am head of Interstellar Travel for G-67235, a small planet in the constellation you Earthlings call Virgo.

This communication is to notify you that one of our lightships will be approaching Earth on May 21, 2013. I wish to formally request landing rights for our ship, which will occur within your country, in the region known as southern Nevada, in the county known as Lincoln.

If all goes well, the ship will be landing at 1:46:55 PM, in "Area 51", a place which has already been used by other XT visitors to your planetary system, and which I thus presume is already known to you and your scientific advisors.

I trust there will be no problems regarding this request.

ZEN

Head of Interstellar Travel

G-67235

P.S. Please use this address for any mail: P.O. Box 672, Pahrump, Nevada 89060

February 28, 2013

Dear Mr. President:

   First off, I did NOT vote for you.
I'd guess that nobody within a radius of
200 miles of here voted for you. The fact
is, I think you're a very weak leader who
happens to know how to deliver a good
speech.

   My question is this: where, and how,
did you learn to get up in front of an
audience and lie so well? Did you take
that Dale Carnegie course, or did you
stand in front of the mirror for a
thousand hours, practicing until you got
it right?

   I have to admit, way back in '08 I
turned off NASCAR a few times to listen
to you. Back then, you could actually
hold my attention for five minutes. But
after four long years of listening to you
rant about everything from outlawing guns
to the evil banks to how we have to help
Israel, I realize now it's all some kind
of magic act, and that your words just
don't add up.

Just look out your office window, Sir. The country's a mess. Not only is the average American barely making it, but Congress has ceased working with you and we're about to plunge into yet another recession. This time, though, it'll be your fault, not Bush's.

Unfortunately, now that you've beaten that fool Romney, who couldn't win a beauty contest in a leper colony, we have to listen to you for another four years, after which time you'll retire back in Hawaii and we'll finally be rid of you. The problem is, I don't know if the country'll last that long.

Sincerely,

Cal Bunker (not my real name)

Gallatin, KY

T.L.P.

Dear Barack Obama:

My name is Turner Pemberton III. I am an attorney and longtime resident of West Palm Beach, Florida, where I have lived for the last 44 years. I am a relatively comfortable person who owns four cats, a golden retriever, as well as two motor yachts, two polo ponies and a 23,000 square foot mansion smack on the intercoastal. I also have a darling wife named Beatrice, four beautiful and talented children, two wonderful granddaughters, and now one great grandchild, soon to arrive.

I am writing to request that you immediately cease and desist in your long and continuing campaign to vilify and demonize, and in general cast aspersions on, those persons in the USA who have become through many years of diligent hard work, extremely wealthy.

Although my father was himself a successful corporate attorney and thus was able to pay my way through Phillips Andover and then law school, I had to work as hard as the next boy. Certainly, Dad's input with Grainger, Steptoe jumpstarted my budding law career, in 1963. But, again, if not for my own considerable hard work and stick-to-it-iveness, as well as endless days sipping martinis with the Grainger "crew", I would never have been eventually invited to become a junior partner in Grainger's Trusts and Estates Planning Division.

Further on in life, I was indeed fortunate to have met my darling and beautiful wife, Beatrice, while on a two-week skiing holiday in Austria. It was love at the sight, and our thirty two years together, here in Florida and at our several homes scattered around the country and in the Caribbean, as well as at my wife's family's estates in Switzerland and France, have been one long paradise on earth.

Sir, I am a proud, lifelong Republican. Speaking objectively, however, I feel our greatest president in the last fifty years was clearly Mr. Nixon, who, despite his occasional anti-Hebraic tirades and paranoid delusional rants, was clearly our most gifted leader, at least intellectually. Sir, it is my opinion that you cannot hold a candle to Mr. Nixon, who if he were alive today would without a doubt finally "do something" -- not only about the thousands of illegals, streaming like rodents across our borders, but also about those pesky Arabs, now infiltrating almost every nook and cranny of our blessed lives.

But enough, as I'm due at the bank and afterward at the club and must run. But, again, please Sir, stop your whining and almost daily invective against the wealthy and those who, through no fault of their own, are highly fortunate. If it weren't for us, nothing, zero, would have ever become of our great and noble Republic.

As always, I reserve the right to notify you again should you decide not to comply with the demand contained in this letter.

Sincerely,

Turner Pemberton Odell

Pemberton, Klieg, Starter & Underhill, PC

West Palm Beach, FL 34098

November 29, 2012

Dear Imposter:

My name's Joe Mumford (not my real name cause I know you'd try to ruin my life by sicking the Secret Service, the IRS, and anyone else you could get a hold of on me.)

I'm writing to let you know I appreciate your sitting there in the Oval Orifice and keeping the seat warm until a white guy shows up who can do the job right. It amazes me how every day you come up with some new lamebrain idea to help either Israel, gays, lesbians, Mexicans (illegal, of course), poor people, or some other minority group with a so-called "gripe", when the real victims in this country are hard-working white men.

It's white men who founded this country way back in 1776, white men who fought and died in the Civil War, WW 1, WW 2 , Korea and even Vietnam (where's Nixon when you need him?), meaning it's white men who made this country great, NOT the weak-kneed complainers listed above.

But hey, somehow you got re-elected, apparently fair and square over that pansy Romney (bless those Latinos, right?), so I guess we have to live with you another four years, then thankfully you'll be gone.

After that, when you've "done your time", if you ever need a job as a security guard I own two gun shops down here in Virginia (The "Heart of the Confederacy"), so send me an application. (ha ha)

Yours not sincerely,

J. Mumford

A "real" American

All mail sorters in the White House must wear gloves in case they have to perform emergency surgery.

TOP SECRET

Office of the Attorney General   *Washington, D.C.*

Memorandum to the President

DATE: January 14, 2010

TO: President Barack Obama

FROM: Eric Holder

SUBJECT: Interrogation of Al Qaeda Operative

You have asked for this Office's report on an interrogation conducted by CIA which took place on ███████████ at ████. You also asked for this Office's views on whether the interrogation technique(s) employed would have violated Section 2340A of Title 18 of the United State Code. Below, is the verbatim CIA report of said interrogation; following, Counsel's views on those techniques as it relates to the statute:

A. Prisoner was tied to a metal chair in a well-ventilated air-conditioned room and repeatedly beaten about the face and neck with a ████ ████████. Prisoner refused to comply with interrogator's demands for answers. Interrogator then switched to a heavy ████████████, which he then employed on Prisoner's ████████ and ███, again repeatedly for several hours, during which time Prisoner screamed in agony until his face began to turn ███. Prisoner eventually regained consciousness, but still refused to comply. When all other methods were unsuccessful, including using a pointed ████ as well as a sharp ████, Prisoner was ultimately forced to watch several hours of *The Brady Bunch TV Show*, as well as a two-hour speech by former President Clinton. This apparently had the desired effect of making Prisoner comply. Prisoner insisted, at first, he was named Abu Ben Akbar, then Akbar Ben Abu, then, finally, Mike Johnson. Prisoner says he had once lived in Cleveland, Ohio, but hated it and moved to Sana, Yemen. Prisoner maintained vehemently he had been only "a messenger" for AQAP (Al Qaeda Arabian Peninsula), but had never seen or met OBL except once in a ███████ parlor in ███████(UAE) sometime in ███████. When threatened again with the TV show, and now obviously under extreme duress, Prisoner admitted that he also was a trained sniper and "former" insurance salesman, but had never lied or bilked anyone while in Yemen, or sold anyone a needless policy. Prisoner was then ███████ again for several hours, then beaten about the ███████ for the hell of it, then returned to his cell.

B. The relevant Code, Title 18, Section 2340A, states: *"Whoever outside the United States commits or attempts to commit torture shall be fined under this title or imprisoned for not more than 20 years, or both, and if death results to any person from conduct prohibited by this subsection, shall be punished by death or imprisoned for any term of years or for life."*

C. Whether Prisoner was in fact subjected to torture by being forced to watch an old TV show is highly subjective, and may ultimately require review by a court with proper jurisdiction. Although the TV show used during interrogation was, and is, extremely bland and wildly dated, and thus could possibly be viewed as torture if watched for more than ten or fifteen minutes, counsel points out that the show has been in syndication for many years and is watched by many people across the country, every day. Thus, the show could be considered amusing, or even highly entertaining, depending on who is watching.

Regarding the second form of torture, counsel deems this action to be much less ambiguous, in that Mr. Clinton tended to drone on endlessly, making listening to a two-hour speech highly annoying, and thus possibly a form of torture, especially when he bites his lower lip.

Eric H. Holder, Jr.
Attorney General

December 31, 2010

Dear President Obama,

Thank you for being such a good president. Someday I hope to come to Washington and take a tour of the White House, and maybe see you and your beautiful wife Michelle as well as Sasha and Malia.

Before that, I had some questions to ask you:

1. Who are some of the most interesting world leaders who have visited you so far?
2. How long did they stay with you in the White House?
3. Did any of them bother you so you had to ask them to leave?

I'm in second grade at the Kensington School and getting all A's, so maybe I'll be president someday, too.

Sincerely,

Jennifer Slotkin, New York, N.Y.

January 28, 2011

Dear Jennifer,

Thanks for both your thoughtful letter and questions. Many interesting leaders have visited the White House during my three years in office. Chancellor Merkel of Germany came once, and was a very colorful lady. Although she spoke only a few words of English and for no apparent reason tended to erupt in a volcano of deep-rooted anger mixed with guilt, she was still fun to have around, especially when she fell over the back of the sofa in the Oval Office onto the canapé table.

Prime Minister Netanyahu of Israel was clearly intelligent and also very funny. On the other hand, he was always whining about the Palestinian people and their aspirations to have their own country, plus how everyone was "out to get" tiny but important Israel, which this year is proudly celebrating its 64th birthday as a democracy. Even when we tried to calm him down with a few beers and by promising to triple (ha ha) our more than generous aid to his small but proud country, he kept on kvetching. Of course, no one's perfect, not even me.

Keep up the good work in school!

Sincerely,

Barack Obama

White House Chief of Staff
Denis McDonough attempts to
hypnotize President Obama during
a critical budget meeting.

CLINTON
FOUNDATION

December 26, 2012

My Friend Barack,

Congratulations on your victory last week over that whopperjawed carpetbagger Mitt Romney. In those final two debates? Hell, ol' Mitt was nervouser than a cat in a room full of rockin' chairs. You beat him fair and square, my friend. And when it was all over? I was grinning like a possum shitting peach seeds.

I knew from the beginning that dog wouldn't hunt, and sure enough, the man went and bought himself a five-gallon bucket o woopass.

Being from Arkansas (or Our-Kansas, as we like to say), I can tell a mile off if a man is straight or catty-wonkered, and in my humble opinion, the man wasn't worth a hoot and a holler. Luckily, you and I are both great leaders of a great country, where people can tell when a man's brains are right side up or ringsidewampis.

You asked me the other day if you should go visit Bibi over in Jerusalem. Well, I've dealt with the man too, and let me tell you, not only was he hit with the ugly stick, he's stubboner than a pig in a mud-pile. Hil said the same thing just the other day, meaning if it were me back in the oval orifice, you dasn't do it. Let the feller sweat, not 'tother way around.

You asked me how I was feeling these days. Well, to tell the truth, I don't feel so good. Frankly, I feel like I was eaten by a chicken and shit off a cliff. And now that I'm pretty much alone up here in Chappaqua (I still don't even know how to *pronounce* the place), I'm hotter than a hen on a hot rock. To make matters worse, the old talleywhacker ain't workin so good neither, so sometimes I feel lower than a snake in a wagon rut.

Other than that, I'm finer'n frog hair and twice as fluffy.

Anyway, as usual Hil's on the rag and on my back about somethin', plus I got to go walk some dog again (third time in the last hour), so I guess I'll close this thang and skedaddle.

Don't forget the envelope with the you-know-what inside for backin' you up at the convention. Hell, I'd do it again for nothin' I had so much fun.

Your pal,

Bill Clinton

April 2, 2013

Dear President Obama,

My name is Cheryl Wczincski. I'm the President of the Women's Book Club of Dayton (Ohio). You may not remember, but you briefly visited our club for a few minutes last October during your final swing through the state.

During that visit, we were able to ask you some questions about the books you were reading. Because of your hectic schedule, however, some of our members still had a number of questions they were unable to ask you.

So, if you don't mind, now that you're back in Washington and probably have a lot more time, here's a list of what I consider the best questions submitted to me:

1. What was the best book you read recently?
2. When and where do you like to read?
3. What's the best book about politics?
4. How big is your personal library and where do you keep it?
5. Where do you keep your most cherished books?
6. What book should every politician read?
7. What books were your favorites growing up as a child?

If you could find the time to answer these questions, all our members would be most grateful. Good luck in your second term!

Sincerely,

Cheryl Wczineski

Cheryl Wczincski, President
Women's Book Club of Dayton

April 30, 2013

Dear Cheryl,

Thanks for your letter regarding my reading habits and my book library. I do remember visiting your club, and the little tapioca-filled pastries you guys made for me.

I had a few free minutes on Air Force One the other day, and was able to write down some answers to your thoughtful questions:

1. The best book I read recently was "Moby Dick". I first read Melville's great whaling saga as a high school sophomore in Hawaii. Knowing I was going to get this question from someone sooner or later, I read it again last month, and it's still as good as the first time I read it.

2. Because I have excellent powers of concentration and nearly photographic recall, I can read almost anywhere. Last week, for example, I read "Fifty Shades of Grey" while shooting skeet at Camp David, then finished it the next day while playing some two-on-two on the White House basketball court.

3. The best book I've ever read about politics is "The Life of Millard Fillmore" by Emerson Babcock, 1927, University of Buffalo Press. This is a little-known book (out-of-print, unfortunately) about a little-known president. Still, I found it to be a real page-turner and recommend it highly.

4. Because every single inch of White House space is reserved for either expensive furniture or 20-something secretaries with great legs (ha, ha), I keep my personal library in a storage closet over at Andrews Air Force Base. It can get pretty loud out there, but for me it's still a great place to read!

5. My most cherished books are under constant guard 24 hours a day by the Secret Service. Regrettably, I can't tell you exactly where because of national security concerns.

6. Any person considering entering politics should read my second book, "The Audacity of Hope". Not only will this increase my royalties, it's also an indispensable primer for anyone who's audacious and for some reason still has hope.

7. My favorite book as a child was "The Island Of Desire" by Robert Dean Frisbie. I used to secretly read this book under the covers at night when I was supposed to be asleep, marveling at Frisbie's humorous descriptions of life in exotic Polynesia. As you may or may not know, Frisbie was from the great state of Ohio, the 'Mother of Presidents'.

I hope these answers prove informative to the members of your club. Enclosed, please find a signed copy of my first book, "Dreams From My Father", which should easily fetch $2,500 on ebay.

Sincerely,

Barack Obama

Corcoran State Prison

March 13, 2011

Dear Leader of Satan's Eternal Army:

Hey, saw you on the idiot box the other day,
giving one of your typical bullshit speeches.
(Yup, they actually let us watch T.V. in here.)
Nothing but lies, Man. Just like Johnson, then
Nixon, then those other phonies in suits who
followed, all world-class liars who spoke nice
but said nothing.

Yep, I'm still in prison, Man ('til 2027),
along with my buddies Juan and Dana. But that
don't mean I'm guilty of anything. I'm only
guilty of being found guilty, by one of your
so-called courts of justice, which serve Satan
but never the people.

Don't worry, I'll be out soon, whatever 'soon'
means. But don't leave the WH light on as it
might not happen for thirty years, or maybe
fifty, or a hundred, or two hundred. Who the
fuck knows?

Even if I die in here, in this crazy pigpen my
father built, more will come who are just like
me. So try as you might, you'll never get rid
of me.

I may sound it, but I am not crazy, just
enlightened. I understand your system and will
use the same corrupt system to escape from my

father's prison, your prison, and take revenge on behalf of my blessed mother. The children you've taught so well to fight in our bloody illegal wars will come back and attack you as well, and the blood will flow like a giant river through hell.

The government has tortured me for 40 years now. Doesn't that give me the right to exact revenge? People who really know, as I do, have no reason to prove they really know to the phonies who think they know.

Forty years ago, being crazy made you different. Today, it makes no difference as everyone's crazy. They just won't know how crazy until it catches up with them one day and the whole rotting system comes crashing down.

Anyway, gotta go to dinner now and eat some slop they call food. By the way, this place sucks the big one. It ain't Kansas, Toto, I'll tell you that.

All the Best,

Charles Manson
ID # B33920

May 22, 2012

Dear President Obama:

Thank you for your recent letter in which you asked me how past presidents have coped with the stress of being president.

U.S. presidents have dealt with the rigors and challenges of governing in a variety of different ways. I believe, however, that President Lincoln offers the most dramatic and distinctive example of how a leader managed to cope in one of the most difficult jobs imaginable.

Although President Lincoln was a highly energetic and very intelligent man, and also very capable, even he was stretched to the breaking point on many occasions, especially during the Civil War years where the survival of the Union was clearly at stake.

As I wrote in chapters 27 and 29 of my eleven-volume biography of the 16th President, 'Lincoln's Beard', in order to alleviate stress, Lincoln, a well-known practical joker, would often resort to pranks, horseplay, and even risqué banter to minimize the strains of governing.

According to the personal diary of Edwin Stanton, Lincoln's Secretary of War, President Lincoln would often stand on his head in a corner of his office for several hours, confounding his staff until gradually they would drift away and go home. At other times, Lincoln would tell jokes at cabinet meetings which he knew weren't funny, waiting to see who among them would make a fool of themselves by laughing. Occasionally, the president would walk into a meeting with his generals wearing only one shoe, his pants inside-out, or his hat upside down, then "falsely admonish" those who "dared to chuckle".

In my opinion, Lincoln's profound sense of humor may have indeed saved his presidency. The only other president to even approach him as far as being entertaining was probably George Washington, another wartime leader whose antics and various japeries were known even in faraway England, and which were compiled by my associate,

Professor Eliot Holcroft, in his recent book, 'Yet Another Book About Washington'.

Best Wishes.

Sincerely yours,

Edwin K. Blankkopf

Edwin K. Blankkopf, B.A., M.A., Ph.D.
Wilford Brimley Professor of American History
Cornell University

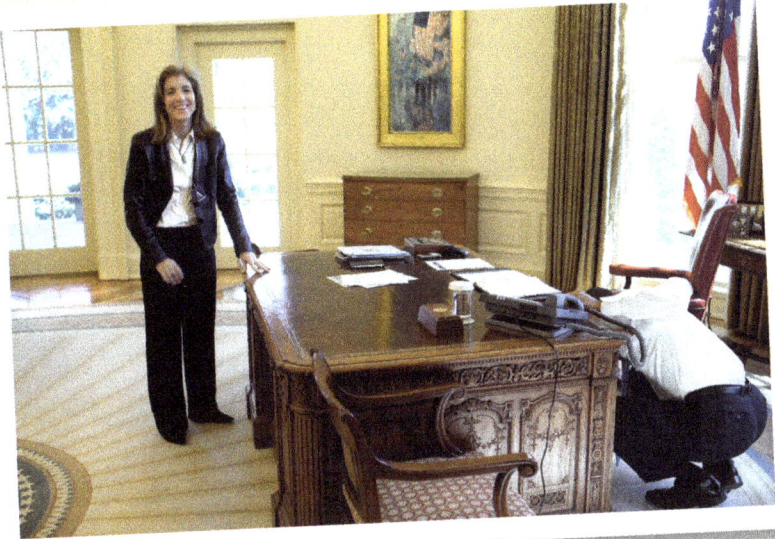

Obama plays hide-and-seek with Caroline Kennedy Schlossberg.

April 8, 2013

Dear President Obama:

I am an average citizen who was recently the victim of a horrible crime which occurred four months ago.

I was walking down my street in a typical tree-lined suburb outside Minneapolis, MN, when a small mob of young dark men assaulted me and my wife. Luckily, I know karate, so I was able to scare them away.

Mr. President, I was one of the lucky ones who managed to escape. Unfortunately, far too many of our citizens are becoming, even as I write this, daily statistics in a new American wave of crime.

For this reason, I would like you to seriously consider the following ideas, which I very strongly feel would reduce crime in our small towns, suburbs, schools, farms, and everywhere else crime occurs:

a. Every citizen over the age of two years should be required to wear a Kevlar bullet-proof vest. Studies have shown this would reduce injuries from crime by 94%;
b. Install electrified barbed wire fences as well as guard towers and machine gun turrets around all schools, malls, movie theatres, and eating establishments. This would not only discourage mentally unstable people from entering, but would help our fence and tower industries;
c. Camps should be placed at strategic remote locations throughout the country where

criminals can be sent right after conviction, <u>before</u> they can appeal. This would ease the overcrowding in our courts, as well as the need to build new prisons, which are extremely costly;

d. Despite what Attorney General Holder said last week, I'm strongly in favor of police having access to the latest in drone warfare. Drones have been highly effective in Afghanistan, and might work on American soil, as well;

e. Capital punishment should be mandatory in all 50 states and Puerto Rico. People found guilty of first, second, and third degree murder should be subject to beheading like in Saudi Arabia, and NOT just lethal injection;

f. Torture is clearly unconstitutional. In some cases, however, like if small children or marijuana is involved, it could be used effectively to extract vital information;

g. A secret police force answerable only to you, Mr. President, should be created to deter and investigate all criminal activity. As its name suggests, this force would act in complete secrecy and have unlimited powers, as long as it's within the law.

I have a list of around 150 more ideas, but I'll save those for another letter as you're most likely busy with other issues.

In the meantime, congratulations on your re-lection, and good luck in your second term!

Yours,

Horst Mueller

Minneapolis, MN

April 2, 2013

Dear President Obama,

My name is Orville Hunnicutt III. I live on my family's farm near Plano, Texas. My grandfather was Lieutenant General Orville Hunnicutt, a decorated veteran of the North Africa campaign during WWII, while my father, Orville Hunnicutt, Jr., bravely and with great valor led a battalion of U.S. Army soldiers at the Battle of Sicily, and as a result was posthumously awarded the Silver Star.

For as long as I can remember, I've been a secret cross-dresser. In case you don't know, cross-dressing involves donning either the clothing, accoutrements, or both, of the opposite sex. Contrary to popular belief, cross-dressing does not necessarily have a sexual motive or connotation behind it, such as homosexuality or some transgender issue. The simple fact is, many men enjoy dressing in women's clothes, and vice versa.

For example, last week a friend and I went to Al's Beef and BBQ dressed in women's clothing. I was wearing a Sea Mistress Mini Dress with belt, and underneath it two-pack lacy booty shorts, while my friend Stewart wore a stretch denim long sleeve blouse with matching pearls.

Tonight for dinner I'll probably change into my favorite: a long sleeve turtleneck bodysuit, while Stewart will no doubt don a sexy schoolgirl tie-top.

I'm writing to you today because you have been in office for almost five years now, but as of yet have made no mention of the fact that many Americans are rabid, albeit secret, cross-dressers. Unlike "shooting skeet", I presume this is because there's still a stigma attached to this activity, forcing almost all of us to remain "in the closet".

In my particular case, I began cross-dressing when I was six years old. Although I've purged (gotten rid of) my collection of women's clothes numerous times, I always start over because I enjoy it so much.

My only wish is that in some small way you could help us by mentioning our group, Cross-dressers of America LLC, at your next State of the Union address, fund-raising gala, or some similar event. It would go a long way toward making all our members just a little bit happier.

Sincerely,

Orville Hunnicutt Odel

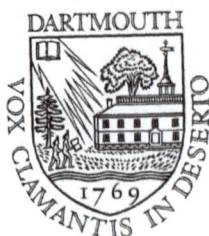

April 2, 1979

Mr. Barry Obama
2115 Punahou Street
Honolulu, HI 96822

Dear Mr. Obama:

The Dartmouth College Admissions Office has completed its evaluation of this year's applicants for admission. It is with sincere regret that I write to inform you that we are unable to offer you a place in the Class of 1983.

I understand that this decision may be a real and profound disappointment to you. I also hope you will realize this is not a reflection on you, but on the outstanding talent represented in the applicant pool. Of the 33,786 individuals who applied, most are clearly capable of doing the work here at Dartmouth. It is truly painful, almost agonizingly so, that we must reject so many outstanding students.

You may be tempted to inquire what was lacking in your application. To be completely truthful, and on the advice of counsel, it is hard for us to point to any specific weakness. Our decision says far more about the microscopic number of places available than about any individual applicant's credentials.

For example, each year Dartmouth reserves 87 percent of its admissions for the children, grandchildren, or great grandchildren of alumni. Another 10 per cent of each year's admissions are reserved for students whose families are extremely generous in their giving to Dartmouth's various building and scholarship funds, with, last year, the average bequest from this category being $526,590; 2.4 percent of the remaining places are reserved for students from Hong Kong who can play the tuba as well as Lacrosse, or from Arizona with an interest in origami. This leaves a total of only four places for applicants like you, extremely hard-working students with a proven track record of outstanding achievement, many of them from highly disadvantaged backgrounds with otherwise little chance of advancement into the elite strata of American society.

Ultimately, however, Dartmouth always seeks to admit those students who demonstrate the most potential to achieve, not only in the highly competitive environment which is Dartmouth, but also in the wider world once they leave school.

While we regret we were not able to respond positively to your interest in Dartmouth, I and my staff wish you every success in your educational pursuits. Experience shows that despite our rejection of you, and the profound sadness, disappointment, and loss of self-esteem this may cause yourself and your family, most of our candidates will most likely be welcomed at other educational institutions, technical or otherwise.

Sincerely,

Ambrose K. Brewster IV

Ambrose K. Brewster IV

Dean of Undergraduate Admissions
AKB/ss

Beaver Crossing, Nebraska

July 17, 2012

Dear Mrs. Obama,

As you are the no-doubt proud mother of two
wonderful girls, I am writing to you this
morning out of profound desperation. My husband
Rick and I have three boys, all of whom are
currently proudly serving in the U.S. Marine
Corps in Afghanistan. Naturally, we're very
proud of them, too, and of their brave service
to our country.

Like you, we also have a daughter, Jennifer,
who's now a senior in high school. Although
she's bright and helpful, Jennie's been
struggling with math, English, history, and
science - actually, with all her courses.

Making matters much worse for all of us,
however, is that Jennie wants to join the
Marines next year too, and fight on the front
lines alongside her three brothers.

Michelle, as you can imagine, Rick and I would
be utterly devastated if our little girl was
ever seriously injured in this long war in
Afghanistan that's been going on for ten years
now. The other day we went to hear some Iraq
and Afghan war veterans who had come to speak
at our local high school. One of the vets had

been horribly injured from an IED; another had lost both legs, and had to be helped onto the stage by his parents. It was a dreadful sight, and so sad. Jennifer was with us and saw those men too, but when we asked her to reconsider her plans later that evening, she insisted that the same thing would "never happen" to her.

The problem, Michelle, is that our young people today have no imagination. They can't see that a steel-jacketed chunk of lead travelling 4,000 feet per second might possibly rip into their fragile young bodies, shattering bone and muscle and killing them instantly, or worse.

Another thing that bothers me, is that very few of our elected leaders have sons or daughters fighting overseas. It's easy to send someone else's child into harm's way, but when it's your own, it's a completely different story.

Assuming Jennie enlists, which she appears at this point one hundred per cent determined to do, I'm equally determined that our little girl be kept out of harm's way. Could you thus please ask your husband to ask Secretary Panetta to somehow bar young women like Jennie from fighting in our armed forces, so that my daughter, and other daughters across America, won't end double amputees -- like those brave men we saw?

          Yours Sincerely,

          Trudy Darlington-Hoyt

March 9, 2013

Dear Mr. President,

As you know, recently I returned from an unofficial trip to North Korea where I was travelling with the Harlem Globetrotters basketball team. Our time in the DPRK was very interesting, and I believe I was able to pick up a considerable amount of information, not only about the DPRK, but also about its young leader, Kim Jong-un.

I spent a total of four days with Mr. Kim, and this is what I'm able to report:

Despite being the relatively young leader of a single-party police state, Mr. Kim in person seems quite open and friendly, and always greeted me with a broad smile. Most importantly, he loves basketball! During our first meeting at one of the many sprawling government ministries which dot the capital, he began screaming at the top of his lungs for no apparent reason, but other than that he was a genial host throughout our visit.

Mr. Kim is clearly beloved by his staff, and swarms of people crowd around him whenever he appears in public. This all seems quite genuine and not staged in any way. The only time I noticed something was wrong, was when two generals were removed from one of several meetings we had, after which I heard loud yelling followed by two quick gunshots. But these may have been unrelated to our meeting, which proceeded without further incident.

The people of North Korea, despite reports to the contrary, seem happy and well-fed. They are always smiling and walk everywhere. Although Pyongyang is a relative beehive of activity, the countryside appears, for some reason, to be completely deserted. On our only trip outside the capital, several corpses lying across the roadway had to be removed, and a number of emaciated farmers begging for food were hustled away by security. Other than this, however, everything seemed OK.

The hotel we stayed at in Pyongyang was surprisingly modern and comfortable. There were concrete stairs leading to the upper floors, and the elevators, when working, had buttons you could push. The only tiny glitch was that the lights and heat remained off most of the time, and thus the temperature in our rooms dropped below freezing for several days. Luckily, there were tons of flashlights and extra blankets, and plenty of lukewarm broth was provided by the hotel staff down in the lobby.

Finally, the food throughout our trip was of the highest order. Consisting often of apparently real beef mixed with rice, it was all very appetizing and abundant. Unfortunately, just after our arrival, Ron, one of our cameramen, developed a severe stomach ailment of some kind, and a producer who began vomiting had to be emergency Medivacked across the DMZ. Other than that, however, the cuisine seemed fine.

Mr. Kim's final words to me on departing were memorable. He said, "Dennis, tell

Obama to call me." I think this is a signal, Sir, that despite their recent nuclear tests and hysterical repeated threats of a preemptive first-strike nuclear attack on the U.S., the DPRK actually wants peace with America, and not war.

Mr. President, I urge you to pick up the phone as soon as possible, and call Kim Jong-un.

Peace,

DR

Dennis Rodman

December 24, 2012

Dear President Obama,

I hate to bother you with this, as you're
probably busier than a one-armed paper hanger.
On the other hand, it's Christmas-eve, I was
alone, and I didn't know who else to write to. (I
haven't used this old typewriter since 'Nam, but
it still works!)

My name's Kyle Sloan. I'm 54 and live in a
trailer park in Hilltop, TX. I got fired from
my job last week at a local laundromat, and am
about to get evicted from my trailer where I
live with my one last friend in life, my dog
Chester. On top of all that, my wife Kiki
finally got sick of all my b.s. and drove off in
the middle of the night with our four kids. I
think they're headed for Mexico 'cause I yelled
at her last month that if she ever tried to take
off with the kids I'd tear her another a--hole
with my AR-15.

If that isn't enough, when I got home last
night, there was a message from my doctor's
office saying the biopsy they did on my colon
was positive and that I have inoperable
advanced stage colon cancer. I just sat on the
floor, opened my last bottle of Jack Daniel's,
and cried for four hours.

Sometimes I think life's a sick meaningless joke,
and that the Lord is playing a giant sick joke
on all of us by throwing disease, crime, war,
poverty, illegal immigration, cancer and all the
rest of it at us God-fearing Americans, and
usually at the worst possible time.

But I don't believe in self-pity, so I'm gonna go
on and try to make a go of things with the time
I have left, which may be only a few weeks.

Anyway, please try to have fun at all those
star-studded inaugural parties, and good luck
in your 2nd term. (And don't worry about
Boehner, Putin & the North Koreans, who're all
a bunch of a-holes if you ask me.)

Sincerely,

Kyle Sloan

May 28, 2013

Dear President Obama:

Thank you for being President of the United States ! I agree with almost everything you say or do, and now that I'm semi-retired I've been able to watch you pretty closely, too. I'm not a politician or even a lawyer like yourself, but despite that I think it's safe to say you've done an excellent job during your four-plus years in the White House.

The only thing I have to complain about, Sir, is something you wrote in your first book, "Dreams From My Father." Although the first part of it was very entertaining, especially the part dealing with your upbringing back in Hawaii, I found it started to drag a bit on page 155, where you're living in Illinois and trying to figure out how to make a difference in society. To tell you the truth, I fell asleep a few times, and even when I picked up the book again the next morning and had drunk three cups of hot coffee (plus a donut) first, the exact same thing happened. For some reason, I haven't been able to get past page 155, even though I've tried as hard as humanly possible numerous times.

Because I thought the problem was me and not your book, last week (even though it was way overdue from the library) I gave it to a good friend of mine, and he had the exact same problem -- he enjoyed the first section, but then on page 155 he got bogged down like I did, and couldn't get started again. Even when I very politely asked him to try, he said 'no way.'

Mr. President, I'm not a professional writer like you and most likely never will be, so I don't know everything, but is there any way an editor somewhere, perhaps on your staff with experience in this area, could go back and simply delete page 155 in your book? I think it'd be a much better reading experience overall, and even those who don't like you as president would find it a lot easier to get through, hopefully all the way to the very end.

Thank you for your time, Sir, and I hope you have a very successful second term.

Best Regards,

Roy Dillard

Elephant Butte, N.M.

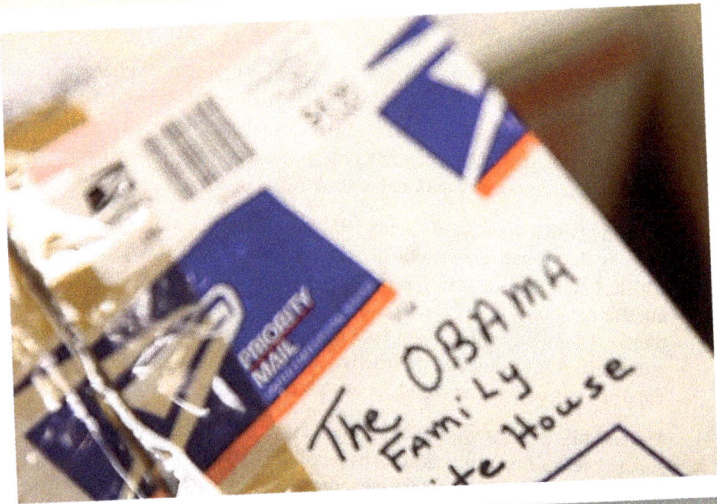

A letter from a typical crackpot is intercepted by the Secret Service.

CHARIOT

CONFIDENTIAL

January 7, 2012

Dear Mr. President,

My name is Edward Teller, Junior. As you may know, my father, an immigrant from Hungary and an integral participant in the Manhattan Project, was the inventor of the hydrogen bomb. Dad passed away in 2003, but will be forever remembered by all who knew him as a staunch defender of our national security.

Working with a small staff in my lab near Stanford, California, I have recently developed a thermonuclear device (see Diagram A, below) which, I believe, is a vast improvement over our current arsenal of nuclear weapons. The " I-650", as we call it, is approximately half the size of our current miniaturized hydrogen warheads -- but at 650 megatons, it's 10 times as destructive. One I-650 could instantly vaporize any city in the world, of any size.

I would like to meet with either you or someone on your national security team, hopefully as soon as possible, to discuss the further development of this important weapon, and to explore how we can work together to incorporate it into our nation's defense arsenal.

Thank you.

Sincerely,

Edward J. Teller, Jr.

Chariot Defense Systems, Inc.

Stanford, California

CONFIDENTIAL

W88 Warhead for Trident D-5 Ballistic Missile

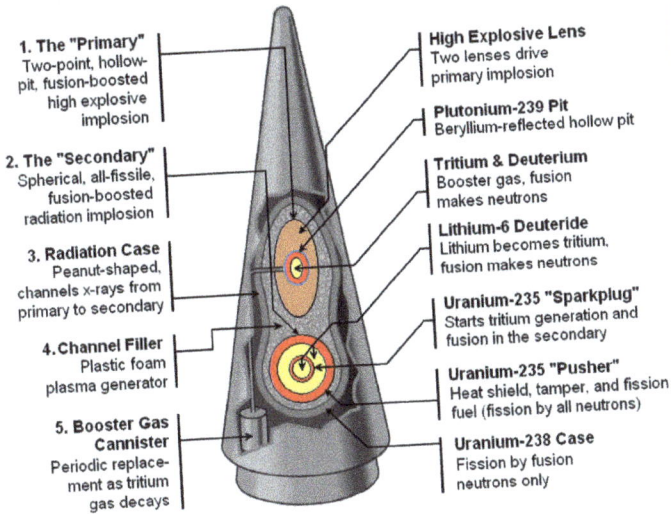

1. The "Primary"
Two-point, hollow-pit, fusion-boosted high explosive implosion

2. The "Secondary"
Spherical, all-fissile, fusion-boosted radiation implosion

3. Radiation Case
Peanut-shaped, channels x-rays from primary to secondary

4. Channel Filler
Plastic foam plasma generator

5. Booster Gas Cannister
Periodic replacement as tritium gas decays

High Explosive Lens
Two lenses drive primary implosion

Plutonium-239 Pit
Beryllium-reflected hollow pit

Tritium & Deuterium
Booster gas, fusion makes neutrons

Lithium-6 Deuteride
Lithium becomes tritium, fusion makes neutrons

Uranium-235 "Sparkplug"
Starts tritium generation and fusion in the secondary

Uranium-235 "Pusher"
Heat shield, tamper, and fission fuel (fission by all neutrons)

Uranium-238 Case
Fission by fusion neutrons only

Diagram A.

Typical foam plasma thermonuclear device. Chariot proprietary alterations include modifications to the High Explosive Lens and the Plutonium Pit. © 2013 Chariot Defense Systems.

THE WHITE HOUSE

WASHINGTON

January 15, 2012

Dear Ed,

Thanks for your letter about your new weapons system. Your father was a great American, and no doubt helped hasten the end of World War II.

To be honest, no one informed me there was an Ed Teller Jr. If I had known, I certainly would have reached out to you earlier.

I've passed your note along to Leon Panetta at DOD. Leon may be leaving the administration soon, but he or his successor will no doubt be intrigued by what Chariot has to offer. We're always looking for new ways to deter our adversaries, and, if diplomacy should fail, completely obliterate them from the face of the earth.

Sincerely

Barack Obama

November 2, 2012

Dear President Obama,

On behalf of the Funeral Home Directors Association of Central Ohio, I would like to thank you for your recent visit to our headquarters in Toledo this past October.

Although your visit was far too short, it was still a definite "shot in the arm" for all of us here who are on the front line of many tragedies, large and small, public and personal, in Ohio and across the nation.

On the brighter side, despite the recent economic downturn and recession, I'm pleased to report that business for our members statewide grew an encouraging 2.4 per cent last quarter and 3.9 per cent nationally. This increase extended all across our own various product lines, from our Immediate "Silver" Cremation Service, which includes a simple cremation and disposal, to our Complete Funeral "Platinum"

Service, a more traditional service which includes family viewing, church service, and burial.

As you know from your visit, in 2009 my own company, Mortimer Funeral Services of Toledo, Inc., received the coveted "Black Umbrella Award" from the National Chapter for its service to the industry.

Ohio, the "Mother of Presidents", along with the Funeral Home Directors Association of Central Ohio, honors your service to our dearly beloved country, and will always reserve a deep soft spot for you and your entire family, especially in this sad time of national recession and grief.

Sincerely,

Karl C Mortimer

Karl C. "Bud" Mortimer

Executive Vice President

Funeral Home Directors Association of Central Ohio

Crawford, Texas

February 34, 2009

Dear Mr. President,

I want to thank you for your saying I was an excellent predssident in your recent state-of-the-union, or maybe it was in a press conf. (I forget), even though I realize you can't say bad things about me cause im an ex-one. I'll try to be nice about you, too, assuming someone asks but I doubt many people will because I'm down here in Texas keeping out of site (heh heh), u know because of all the problems I cawzed. Also, I keep getting these hate mails from people all over America who think I was a bad leader so I sorta have to keep my head down these days.

Im having a ball (heh heh) down here in hot-as-bejesus Texas, that is when I can get away from Laura whoze afraid I'll go nutz from all the spare time we both have, altho she has a lot less than I do cause she has to do the dishes now that the white-house help aint around any more . ☹

Starting in May I'll be up in Kennebunkport at my parents house, as usual, so if you want to visit and go on a boat ride with us, you can, just tell me what time, OK?

Anyway, good luck in the Fishbole, and let me know if you need any help with anything.

Yours,

George W Bush

P.S. I left some gum in the top drawer. You can have it if you want..

10000 Memorial Dr. Suite 900

Houston, TX 77024

March 20, 2009

Dear Mr. President,

On behalf of Barbara and myself, I would
like to apologize for the letter that our
son George recently sent you, dated
February 2009.

For many years, we've tried to get George
not only to use a typewriter, but also,
more importantly, to "think things
through" before embarking on some wacky
escapade, such as writing a letter to his
successor in the White House, which, if it
somehow fell into the wrong hands could be
highly embarrassing to all concerned.

This is certainly not George's first
mistake. As you know, I was vehemently
opposed to our country's harebrained
incursion into Iraq in 2003, and very
firmly communicated my ideas on this to W.
during a family picnic in Kennebunkport.
In retrospect, it is abundantly clear to
me now that the partial inebriation George
was suffering from during that happy June
event (Barb's 77th), as well as Rove's

highly effective brainwashing techniques, caused him to ultimately disregard my advice and forge ahead with his cockamamie scheme.

I'll admit to you now, I presume in the strictest confidence, that unlike his brother Jeb, George has always been somewhat of a problem child. Barb and I have through the years spared no expense, from his schooling at Andover and Yale, to various investment schemes we supported (and which thankfully never came to light), all in the hope George would never besmirch the good Bush name. Sometimes we succeeded, other times we did not, and I blame myself entirely for both the failures as well as the successes.

Assuming my health remains intact, I trust we'll see you and Michelle again in the near future.

Until then, stay well.

All the best,

June 30, 2012

Dear President Obama,

I have been living in a dark hole under my parents' basement for sixteen years. Despite this, I understand molecular biology and advanced calculus, and can play the accordion while blindfolded. I accomplished all this in total darkness without any help from anyone.

Because of these accomplishments, I was thinking of applying for a grant from some world-famous foundation, like the MacArthur or Ford Foundations, or possibly even The National Endowment for the Arts. Unfortunately, I would need someone important to nominate me first, and not someone like my Uncle Fern who's an optician and who hates my guts anyway.

My question , Mr. President, is this: would you consider nominating me for one of these awards, because if you did and I won one we could split the award money fifty-fifty, which could add up to a lot even after we split it, and which I understand would be "unrestricted" in that you could use it for anything you want, like, for example, a new office at the White House or possibly a luxury condo for your daughters when they grow up.

Thanks for reading my letter.

Sincerely,

E. C. "Ed" Grimmick
Buffalo Gap, S.D.
Tel: 605-555-2774

From: clemF@voiceprint.net

Sent: Friday, March 01, 2013 2:38 PM

To: B.Obama@whitehouse.gov

Subject: Help!

Dear President Obama:

My name's Clem Fulmer. The other day my girlfriend broke up with me, so I decided to come out here to Bryce Canyon with my trail bike to let off some steam. Problem is, for some reason I'm now hanging on for dear life on this crag (near Bristlecone Loop) meaning if someone (like with the Park Rangers) don't get here soon and throw me a rope I'm definitely a gonner.

My father always told me honesty is the best policy, so I'll just admit now I didn't vote for you and never wood, but I'd sure like some help anyway!

Thanks,

Clem

Sent from my iPhone

THE WHITE HOUSE

WASHINGTON

From: B.Obama@whitehouse.gov

Sent: Saturday, March 9, 2013 11:22 PM

To: clemF@voiceprint.net

Subject: Help!

Dear Clem:

Bryce Canyon National Park is a historic landmark. The area around Bryce became a National Monument in 1923 and was designated as a National Park in 1928. It's cool you ride your trail bike there and can take advantage of our country's natural scenic beauty!

Sincerely,

Barack Obama

October 11, 2012

Dear Darling Barry:

I know we haven't properly communicated since you left Harvard and law school, but I feel, deep in my heart and after thinking about it for over thirty years, that now is the time for me to speak to you once again.

As you know, we were quite close during those tender years when we were in torts together. I recall fondly the hours we spent studying on the floor in my room, (sometimes in my little single bed), then afterwards taking long walks under the grey Cambridge sky, discussing Kant, Heidegger, Hawaii, and Palsgraf vs. Long Island Railroad.

Dearest, you were so idealistic in those days, but in the thirty years that have since passed under our bridge, I've noticed a significant change, and not for the better. Now, it seems, no doubt due to your overly cautious nature which up to now has served you so well throughout your career, you sometimes get bogged down in an endless analysis of a situation, instead of taking the bull by the horns and doing something.

This brings us to my current situation. To make a long sad story very short, after our little "tryst" in the Holmes laundry room, I was as you know forced to withdraw from school -- not because of what we did there, which was an act of passion and love (I trust on both our parts), but because my father Earl (who died six years ago in a boating accident) was soon experiencing financial difficulties back in Chippewa Falls and I was forced to withdraw from school.

Little Jack (named after my grandfather) is now big Jack, a handsome young man of twenty-two, and is working hard at his job at a downtown Racine copy shop. The trouble is, because he was born with a severe learning disability and therefore relies on me heavily, I'm seriously short of funds right now. I know both your books were wildly successful; so, could you see your way clear to sending us some money - specifically $35,000 via certified check by next Thursday?

As stated above, I've thought about this letter and what I would say in it for many years. It's possible that by the time you're finished reading it, I may have already regretted writing and sending it. I'm doing this only for our love-child, and not in any way to get back at you for being cold and dismissive when I told you about him those many years ago.

You don't have to bring me up to date, of course, as I know what's been happening with you, the kids, and Michelle, who I adore, and, I admit it, envy profoundly.

This is absolutely not not not a form of blackmail: it is very simply a silent cry from someone who loved you as much as any woman could, who still does, and always will.

Love,

Therese

January 23, 2009

Dear Mr. President:

My name is Mary Wanahalipani. Up to seven weeks ago, I was a clerk in the Department of Health - Vital Records Department for the State of Hawaii. I had been an employee in good standing there for close to 11 years, and had never been guilty of any institutional infraction whatsoever.

In August 2008, I was asked by my supervisor, Mr. Steve Watapahalu, to pull your birth certificate from our paper files. After spending three fruitless days searching, I found no record of your birth in the State of Hawaii. The following afternoon, I was called into Mr. Watapahalu's office, and was informed that I was being immediately terminated due to "insubordination, poor attendance, and a less than satisfactory overall job performance."

Mr. President, I have three teenaged kids and an elderly mother who lives with us. I am the sole breadwinner of my family as my husband Regis was killed when he fell into a pineapple processor, three years ago. I feel my termination was completely unjustified, and obviously a result of not finding a certificate that in fact never even existed. Later that month, I saw on the internet a document that Nancy Pelosi and

Senator Schumer claimed was your Hawaii birth record, but I never found this same document when I looked myself, and so I strongly believe it is a <u>complete forgery</u>.

Mr. President, I believe a serious injustice was done to me, and therefore, before I call a reporter I know at KITV in Honolulu, could you please have someone in the White House contact my employer and ask them to kindly re-hire me?

Thank you for your immediate attention to this request.

Sincerely,

Mary Wanahalipani

Mary Wanahalipani

Honolulu, Hawaii

november 9 th. 2012

sir:

congratulations for you that is whereas for me

well i'm not so good myself i mean with all

these meds i have to take every day and that

damned crazy puppy i read your kids are trying

to find plus these headaches are driving me

absolutely bonkers even though i already am—

anyway i'll try to stick to the point if there is

one which i doubt which there is for the last two

years or maybe more   i've been trying to get my

lawyer to sue the secret service for spying on me

back when i lived in berkley in the late 70's but

dammit the man won't comply, and even

when i ask my family for help they won't call

me back even collect but just tell me i'm

'hopelessly delusional' and that's a direct quote

when they visit which isn't often maybe twice a

year which i think is terrible seeing in my entire

life so far i never hurt even a fly. i was pretty

smart back then with an iq well off the charts

(or so they tell me), and even got my phd in

astrophysics in record time, but then the circuits

got sort of overloaded what with the drugs and

all and well the whole thing just fell apart

overnightubut hell the point here is if i don't get

out of this hellhole so i can see my lawyer who

also doesn't visit me and real soon believe me

something bad's gonna happen, not just to the

usa but maybe the whole world if you know

what i mean. how do i know this? i know

because these space aliens with giant heads and

tiny eyes communicated it to me through the

walls here which are three feet thick which tells

you how powerful they are. anyway, the men in

the white coats are heading this way so i'll stop

writing and say good-luck to you, sir, for the rest

of your time on this godforsaken sphere called

planet earth.

sincerely,

ed starcher, phd

bryce state hospital, tuscaloosa, al

June 8, 2012

Dear Mr. President:

As a small farmer living in rural Idaho, I don't have much time to talk to people about what's happening with our country. The reason is, I spend most of my time working hard on my family's twenty-acre spread, as well as bringing up six kids with my wife Jessie, who I've been married to for 22 years.

As a mature adult, however, I've had plenty of time to think about a lot of the issues confronting our country, and have developed some opinions about a lot of them. Below, is just a partial list of the many issues we currently face here in the USA:

1. The Economy: Too many people are freeloading and not paying their own way. For this reason, I would immediately eliminate Medicaid, Food Stamps, Head Start, Aid for Families with Dependent Children, as well as all foreign aid except aid to Great Britain, our closest ally, plus a number of other programs too numerous to go into here. I am not against all federal programs, however. Medicare, for example, is a good one which helped my Dad get through a recent bout with pneumonia. Also, Social Security should be maintained for the same reason.

2. Abortion: I would abolish abortions under any circumstances, even in the cases of rape and incest. I have always believed that life begins when a man and woman are married, even if no child results.

3. Marijuana: Marijuana is clearly a product of the devil and the liberal left. It should thus be kept a serious criminal offense equal to first degree murder. I have never used this drug personally, but I have heard it can

cause serious side effects, such as mental
illness and even rabies.

4. <u>Stem cell research</u>: I haven't studied the
science involved in this, beyond what I've
read in Reader's Digest. However, it seems
the money now being used for this could be
put to much better use, such as in
agricultural price supports and, eventually,
putting men on Mars.

5. <u>Gun rights</u>: I strongly believe it is the
right of every legal American citizen over
the age of eight to bear arms. I say eight
because that's when I taught my son Chris to
use a gun, and except for the accidents at
the playground 2 years ago and then at the
silo, he's had no problem at all learning to
use one responsibly.

6. <u>Minimum wage</u>: I think many of our corporate
leaders deserve to receive a minimum wage of
at least $100,000/yr. I know that probably
sounds high, but it's based on what it costs
now to have a decent home, two nice cars, and
put two kids through college. As far as
workers' pay, that should be left up to the
employer. If he can afford to pay a dollar an
hour, that's fine with me as long as it
doesn't affect our economy.

7. <u>Afghanistan</u>: All of our national budget
should be directed toward eliminating the
Taliban! If this means our economy will
permanently suffer and possibly go bankrupt,
it doesn't matter. National defense should
always be priority #1.

8. <u>Israel</u>: Israel is a strong country. It has
shown it can handle its many Arab enemies
pretty well without us butting in. For that
reason, they should not need any more money
from us, ever.

9. <u>Homeland Security</u>: I hate to see anybody,
especially a farm animal, being tortured or
harmed in any way. However, if an Arab enemy
is believed to have information about an

impending attack on our soil, they should
have their skin ripped off with a chisel
plow, then hung upside down in a grain
elevator until they confess. 9-11 must never
be repeated, especially in our great country.

Anyway, Sir, those are just some of the topics
I've thought about in the past couple of years.
You may not agree with all or even some of
them, but at least you've seen them assuming
your staff hasn't intercepted this letter.

Good luck in your next four years!

        Sincerely,

        Mike Buttram

        Culdesac, Idaho

President Obama surprises Michelle in White House kitchen on Halloween night.

July 14, 2011

Dear Mr. President Obama,

My name is Miguel Sanchez Ortega. In 1986, my young family decided we would try to go to America from our home in Guatemala. In Guatemala, we were desperately poor. With no money, the only way to get to the U.S. would be by walking, and using the many dangerous cargo trains that move northward through Mexico.

One dark night in 1986, all of us began the long journey from our small home in Zacapa. The trip north was difficult, and also very dangerous. Bands of thieves twice robbed us near Veracruz, where all of our food and personal belongings were taken from us at knifepoint. Despite this, me and my wife Maria, along with our six young children, somehow managed to continue our journey, the dream of America floating before our eyes.

Day and night, we walk northward. Eventually, we arrived at the border with the USA. Waiting until midnight, we slipped under the border fence at Jacumba, avoiding detection by hiding in a large sewage pipe, where all of us huddled together for three nights, terrified and with no food or water. My daughter, Maria, became ill, and my son Miguel Jr. came down with a serious infection from which he almost died.

After walking for nine days across the broiling southern California desert, with God's grace we eventually found ourselves on the outskirts of San Diego. Using a quarter I found on the ground, I called my cousin Pablo, who picked us up two hours later. Pablo brought us to his home, a tiny one-bedroom apartment, where he fed and sheltered us for twenty months until me and my family were able to find an apartment of our own in another town not far away.

After working in a laundry for six years, and saving every penny I earned, I opened a small tire repair shop. My sons and I worked very hard day and night, and also learned English, so that today, seventeen years later, I am the proud owner of five tire shops. Two of my sons, Jose and Miguel, Jr. are in medical school at UCLA, and my daughter Maria just had another grandson for us, our fifth. Most importantly, we are all proud citizens of the United States of America!

Mr. President, I am writing today with tears in my eyes concerning a new problem. I was informed last month by the U.S. Immigration Department that my citizenship is being revoked, and that I will be soon deported back to Guatemala. The reason I was given, Sir, is that when I wrote my street address on my citizenship application, instead of writing 44682 Pacifica Blvd, I somehow left off the "2" at the end. The government says that I "fraudulently misrepresented" my personal information, and for this reason I am being immediately deported.

Mr. President, the reason I left off the "2" on my application was because I was so excited I was soon to become a citizen of this great country. I would've forgotten <u>my own name</u> if Maria hadn't calmed me down in the car first.

My lawyer has told us there is nothing he can do to help me. I have written to Senator Boxer, Senator Feinstein, as well as Leader Pelosi and all our congressmen and congresswomen, but none of them responded to any of my 209 letters or 316 follow-up phone calls.

If you could possibly in some way intercede for me, for my family, Mr. President, I would be truly grateful. Otherwise, I will be on a bus back to Guatemala City next Thursday, the 21st, at noon. Me and my family are depending on you to help us, or all that I've done to escape grinding poverty, raise a family, become a citizen, and live the American dream, will have been for no reason. Gracias!

Yours Sincerely,

Miguel S. Ortega

Miguel Sanchez Ortega, Prop.

ORTEGA TIRE REPAIR, INC.

87364 Valencia Blvd. (rear)

San Diego, Ca. 92101

THE WHITE HOUSE

WASHINGTON

April 9, 2013

Dear Mr. Ortega,

Thank you for your letter regarding the problems you're having with the Department of Immigration. Everyone hates paperwork!

The U.S. Government is a huge, sprawling bureaucracy, and I can imagine how difficult your situation must be for you and your family.

As you know, I have submitted a number of bills to Congress which would have solved many of the problems you're now encountering. Sadly, all were blocked by the Republicans, an intransigent mob of vengeful old men with no serious interest in immigration reform. And now that the Sequester is in effect, things will only get a lot worse.

Please remain hopeful, and don't lose faith in the American dream.

Sincerely,

Barack Obama

May 28, 2012

Dear President Obama:

My name is Jennifer Strawbeck. I live in Kermit, West Virginia where I am a happily divorced mother of three boys: Clyde, Owen, and Franklin, all of whom attend Kermit Elementary School.

Last Tuesday Clyde, who's seven, was sent home early from school when they found he'd stolen a dollar from another boy during recess. Not only did they send Clyde home, but the local Sheriff sent a man out later that same day to investigate. Clyde was kinda sleepy from all the commotion at school, and I guess they didn't like his answers because they put him in handcuffs (!), then brought him down to the police station. When I tried to bring him home later, they said he had to stay overnight "as a precaution".

Mr. President, what kind of country are we living in where a seven year old boy has to spend a whole night in jail for stealing a dollar? I could understand it if he'd stolen more, or if he had gone on a rampage and KILLED someone with one of those 40-bullet assault rifles. But merely stealing a dollar then going to jail for it just seems flat-out crazy.

A lawyer was able to get Clyde returned to us, (the lawyer cost me $2,340, which I had to borrow from my sister) but I'm wondering whether to send him back to school or simply teach him at home.

My question to you, Pres. Obama, is: if there's anything you can do to prevent things like this happening again in the future, Clyde and I'd sure appreciate it.

Sincerely,

Jennifer Strawbeck

Kermit, W. Virginia

THE WHITE HOUSE

WASHINGTON

September 30, 2012

Dear Jennifer:

It would appear that the authorities may have overreacted by, first, arresting your son, then, second, keeping him in jail overnight. Luckily Clyde wasn't sent to prison or, God forbid, executed.

Senator Chuck Schumer of New York introduced a bill in Congress last year which would have prevented something like this from occurring, but it was defeated, 99-1. All we can do is to keep trying and hopefully things will change for the better.

Sincerely,

Barack Obama

March 23, 2012

Dear Mr. President Obama:

My government has received your letter of January 3rd regarding your request to "open a new dialogue" and to "reset" the relations between your country, the United States of America, and the Democratic People's Republic of Korea.

Unfortunately, the great people of the DPRK must strongly and forcefully reject this insulting request.

The glorious Democratic People's Republic of Korea will in a thousand years never agree to any request for normalization with the Capitalist Empire and its lackey cohorts until the U.S. ceases its economic and military support of all of the various puppet entities whose sole purpose is the destruction and impoverishment of our great and glorious country.

The evil puppet master, the United States of America, and its head puppeteer, you Mr. President Obama, must first unconditionally agree to reconsider its evil view of our great and glorious people, who you and your State Department continue to slanderously refer to as the 'Hermit Kingdom', who have been struggling under harsh economic sanctions for the last sixty eight years since its founding by our Great Leader, Kim Il-Sung; and who, despite these terrible hardships, are about to win a glorious victory in their never-ending fight against those satanic puppet regimes aligned against it.

If America and its marionette stooges should choose to stupidly ignore this warning, burning fires of terrible consequence will be sent to the south, and elsewhere, with many deaths and utter destruction for those who join the forces of the arch-puppeteer regime, the United States of America.

Sincerely,

Kim Jong-un

Democratic People's Republic of Korea

March 31, 2013

Dear Mr. President,

Firstly, I would like to congratulate you on your re-election this past November. As a perennial winner myself, I think I know precisely the elation and pride you must be feeling as a result of your victory.

As you no doubt know, Mr. President, due to alleged doping offenses, the U.S. Anti-Doping Agency has recently stripped me of all my racing awards and banned me from professional cycling for life. This has been the source of considerable disappointment and heartache for me, but I am doing my best to come to terms with the situation I now find myself in.

Not only have these actions by the ASADA hurt me professionally, they have also been hurtful to my family, as well as to those who have supported me throughout my career. They have also seriously besmirched the Armstrong family name. As you know, Neil Armstrong, a distant cousin of mine, was the first man to step on the moon.

Mr. President, despite what you've been hearing about me in the press and on TV, there's a simple explanation for all of it. I'd like to offer that explanation to you now.

In June of 2009 I was living in Paris, preparing for another run at the Tour de France. It was early summer, the weather in Paris was warm and welcoming, and I was excited about my return to competitive bicycling.

As I was walking back to my hotel late one night after an intimate dinner with friends, I was suddenly waylaid by two men. My assailants covered me with a blanket, and then roughly threw me into the back of a van. As the van raced away into the night, first my hands and feet were bound, then I was blindfolded. At the same time, I heard the men talking; their voices were not French or American but Middle Eastern, perhaps even Russian or central Asian. As you can imagine, in my agitated state I couldn't think straight, and felt that death would visit me at any moment.

Approximately an hour later, the van I was in stopped abruptly. I surmised I was now at some kind of airfield, as soon I heard the unmistakable sounds of jets taking off and landing. Several minutes later I was placed on an aircraft, which then took off for points unknown. I was seated in this aircraft for several hours, all the while remaining bound and blindfolded, with no communication or explanation from any of the people responsible for my plight. After several hours of sightless boredom, I was finally offered a drink and a snack, but I declined as I wanted to concentrate on how to escape my captors.

We were airborne for perhaps six hours, until finally we landed. Once again I heard the same foreign voices as I was removed me from the aircraft, placed in a car, then whisked away. For an entire day, or possibly even two, I remained in this auto, wondering where I was, and how much longer I had to live. Again, because of my blindfold, I could not accurately tell at any point if it was day or night. Due to a steady rush of hot wind across my face, however, I was able to surmise I was now in some tropical climate, perhaps Arabia, or even further south in darkest Africa.

Several more days passed, until due to a lack of food or even water I eventually fell unconscious. When I regained consciousness sometime later, I discovered I was sitting, still bound, in a chair. My blindfold had been removed, and thus I was able to see I was now in a large room, in some kind of ornate palace out of the Arabian Nights. A window was open nearby, and when I focused on what was beyond it I saw gently swaying palm trees and, further on, a sere landscape suggesting a place bordering the nether regions of the Sahara.

Eventually, one of the many ornate doors opened, and into this room entered a beautiful young woman. She approached quickly, then, kneeling before me, told me in a hushed whisper her name was Nasri. Nasri informed me that, indeed, I had been abducted, and that I was now the prisoner of Kafir, the Sultan of Jubaal. Nasri then informed me that Kafir was not only unimaginably wealthy, but also a bicycling enthusiast currently very ill from a rare form of gout, and that his dying wish was to see me, the greatest competitive bicyclist in the world, race around his palace before he expired.

Nasri asked me if I would do this, to which I replied very firmly in the negative, explaining that, because I was being held against my will, I would not, like some trained seal, perform for the Sultan. Further, I demanded to be released immediately and taken (at the Sultan's expense) back to France.

Returning to my room the following morning, Nasri told me the Sultan was very angry I had rejected his demand. At this point, she removed all her clothes and attempted to make love to me. Fortunately, I had already used the dinner knife from my previous night's meal to cut through the ropes holding me and was able to jump out the closest ornate window, just behind me. I fell for several seconds, convinced I was going to die at any moment, and certainly when I landed. Fortunately, my fall was interrupted by a large palm tree, which clearly saved my life.

Just under the palm was a gently flowing river the color of aquamarine, which soon carried me away from the Sultan's palace. For several days I floated down the river, all the while clinging to a small piece of Styrofoam, during which time I witnessed many local nomads and camel drivers travelling along its banks, no doubt bringing their various wares to distant markets.

After floating for several days, the river deposited me at the edge of a small desert outpost, a mostly uninhabited speck in the middle of nowhere called Habash. Making my way into the center of town, I boarded an air balloon operated by a bearded local who called himself Amahl. As I gazed at the brown desert wastes passing below me, Amahl's balloon carried me another hundred miles, most likely eastward, until a day later we landed at yet another uninhabited outpost. Directing me to a taxi service he owned there, Amahl offered to chauffeur me an additional three hundred miles, a proposition which I agreed to, until finally we arrived at a tiny oasis known as Rootintootin, which, by sheer luck, happened to feature a small regional airport.

Thanking Amahl a thousand times, I took the first flight out, and by way of Istanbul found my way back to Paris, where I was able to rent a bicycle at the airport and peddle my way back to my hotel. I ate a hearty meal, slept for several days, then awoke and considered my options. Not one to be defeated easily, a week later I came in third in that great spectacle known as the Tour de France.

Unfortunately, Sir, and as you can imagine, my abduction took a great toll on not only my body but also on my psyche. Several weeks following this adventure, I was directed to a famous psychiatrist, Dr. Otto von Putzstein, recently of Vienna, who informed me that, no doubt due to my horrific ordeal and subsequent escape, I was suffering from PTSD, for which the doctor prescribed a number of strong medications which he said I should take to counteract the effects of not only "extreme anxiety", but also a mild case of malaria I had apparently contracted during my voyage down the river.

Mr. President, this is my story, and also my explanation for why the USADA found drugs in my body, and also why I now find myself ostracized and an outcast in the world of professional bicycling, probably forever. I am not a bad person; I am merely a victim of circumstances obviously not of my own choosing. I know it will be difficult, but, seeing you now know the whole truth, I am hoping you can find a way not only to forgive me, but also to help me regain my good name, as well.

In the meantime, please give my love to your family, and good luck in your second term.

All the best,

Lance Armstrong

President Obama is almost swept away by six-inch wave in Hawaii.

October 15, 2012

Dear Mr. President,

Thanks so much for inviting Sylvia and me to spend a weekend with you and Michelle at Camp David. We both had a wonderful time. It was great seeing Sasha and Malia having so much fun there; they appeared to really enjoy themselves.

I very much appreciated our in-depth discussions about the future of our country, and, on the personal side, my future at DOD. My thirteen months as Defense Secretary have been some of the most gratifying of my entire career in government. I've been extremely proud to serve you, your administration, and our blessed country.

On Saturday night, during our hotly contested game of "Battleship", you asked that I consider staying on for a second term as Secretary of Defense. Although I very much appreciate your offer and your continuing faith in me, after careful consideration and consultation with Sylvia, my family, and my accountant, I've decided to move on with my life and return to the old walnut farm in California.

The reasons for my decision are partly personal and partly professional. The primary reason is that during the past year or so I've grown tired of the drive in the limo from my townhouse all the way over to DOD each morning. Quite frankly, it's a schlep. The traffic can be horrible at that time of the day, and is getting a lot worse, very quickly. Last week my chauffeur got a $200 speeding ticket when I was in danger of missing a critical early-morning meeting with JCS.

The problems don't end there, however. It takes me nearly six minutes to walk from my DOD office to the Pentagon cafeteria. Once in the cafeteria, not only is the lighting bad, but the place is downright drafty, even cold. More importantly, the chef salad there tends to be limp, and on several occasions the milk had gone bad, ruining my daily noon cup of coffee. I also once ate a chicken salad sandwich with a small bone in it. I also strongly feel there could be a much wider choice of yogurts in the dairy case. Right now, despite my multiple complaints to the Navy Exchange Service Command, the Pentagon cafeteria still offers <u>no low-fat yogurt</u>.

On the home front, things are getting harder too. Although we have a staff of four at our beautiful residence, Sylvia has indicated she's unhappy with the amount of natural light in the living room, as well as with the size of our heated exercise pool. She's also confessed that the service at her beauty salon has deteriorated significantly in the past year or so, and reminded me that it takes almost half an hour to get to Marcel's, our favorite French restaurant.

Overriding all these considerations, however, is the issue of my salary. My financial advisers have indicated to me that, heading into retirement back in Carmel, we'll need a minimum income of approximately six and a half million dollars a year to maintain any modicum of comfort once we return to California, which we'll obviously do eventually. This would absolutely not be attainable at my current salary of $199,700.

Again, thanks for your kind offer, and for your trust in my service to you and the entire DOD family. In the meantime, I look forward to seeing you, Michelle and the girls again soon, hopefully at your Inauguration !

All the Best,

Leon Panetta

Beneath the famous portrait of George Washington, First Lady Michelle Obama participates in a wacky sack race against TV personality Jimmy Fallon.

August 15, 2011

Dear Honorable Sir:

It is with great esteem and humbleness that I write to you today, Sir, hoping and trusting that you are comfortable in your large abode in that great city known as Washington, DC.

My name, Sir, is the Honorable Nigel Mkwekwe. Currently, I am a resident in longstanding of the beautiful ancient metropolis known as Lagos, in Nigeria, where the Nigerian people honor you daily by their close attention to all you do and say while leading that great and honorable country, the United States of America.

Sir, it is with equally great happiness that I am able to inform you through this letter, that at one period in my relatively uneventful life, before I was forced to suddenly take up residence here in this beautiful but crowded country, I was a citizen of that almost equally wonderful country known as Kenya.

My life in fact started there, in 1963, in the small town of Kwangwari. It is with sincere and everlasting gratitude to the Lord above, that during my considerable time there I became employed as a lowly bicycle messenger in my family's business, The Mkewkwe Taxi Service, located in Nairobi, hand-delivering messages to and from the highly esteemed members of the Kenyan Government.

It was during my tenure as a messenger that I was infinitely fortunate to have struck up a brief but highly satisfying friendship with a gifted economist employed by the government, whose surname was "Obama". The facts are these: this man and I met late one night at one of the many popular cafes on Mkwekwe Street (named after my great great grandfather Cyrus Mkwekwe) and from then onwards over a period of nine weeks spent many a night discussing, among other things, economics, maths, astronomy, the weather, as well as whatever it was the papers were printing. Citizen Obama, I was to learn much later, was none other than your father, Barack Obama Sr., who we all know passed away in 1982 in, apparently, a very unfortunate as well as tragic auto accident.

My letter today is to ask you, very humbly, Sir, if there is any way possible you could be of great assistance to me and my family, which numbers now nine including seven little children, all being looked after by their loving mother, Jimpali. You see, like yourself, I am a hardworking man too. Regrettably, late last year, I met with some misfortune when my fine auto was hit broadside by a large truck in downtown Lagos. Fortunately, with some luck and quick thinking, I was able to bring suit in the local courts, subsequent to which I was awarded 12,000,000 Nigerian naira (US $72,000.), an amount now sitting, unused, in the Central Bank of Nigeria.

Mr. President Obama, is there any way you could possibly assign one of your staff, or perhaps a member of your venerable immediate family, to wire the same amount stated above to a Swiss bank of your own choosing, attention the Manager there, and to my own credit? Once this is done, I have been informed and assured by the CBN President, Mr. N. Nakrulu, that the funds in the CBN would be freed and placed at your immediate disposal, including a nice commission added on equal to ten per cent (10%) of the aforementioned amount.

I have attempted to engage others to help us free these funds, but I am but a small unconnected merchant. However, considering my close friendship with your esteemed father, however brief, it is my hope you could overlook this and assist a man, husband, and father in great and dire distress.

I remain,

Very Truly Yours,

Hon. Nigel Mkwekwe

27 Thomas Salako Street

Ikeja, Lagos, Nigeria 23401

President Obama searches for someone to talk to at a White House gathering.

September 4, 2012

Dear Mr. President,

My name is Kell Burridge. I live in a small
trailer on the outskirts of Homer, Nebraska.
For thirty five years I was a security officer
at the home of Homer Textiles, which I
recently retired from. I didn't want to retire
but they made me, plus I have a bad left eye
which is acting up.

My question is: What's it like living in a
big place like the white house? I saw some
pictures of it in this old copy of National
Geographic I found in my storage locker
recently and it looked pretty impressive. It
looked like it went on forever with all these
different rooms like the Lincoln bedroom and
the East and West wings, etc. I guess you
even have your own private bowling alley (now
a basketball court?). So, these are my
questions:

1. How long does it take to get to the Oval
   Office from your bed? I hope not long.
2. If the WH chefs cook something you hate, like
   some fancy asparagus recipe, can you send it
   back, or do you have to eat it anyway?
3. Can your kids roam around and go anywhere, at
   any time, or do they have to abide by certain
   rules, like staying out from behind your desk
   during a national crisis?

4. Does Michelle have to pitch in with the cleaning, or can she just stay in bed all day and watch TV? (like me!)
5. How many square feet do you guys have? I have about 230, which is OK unless my girlfriend Bernice comes over, which is a lot now that she's laid off from the chemical plant.
6. When dignitaries visit you, do they have their own bathrooms or do they have to use yours? And can't that cause some embarrassment if everyone "has to go" at the same time?
7. I saw on TV what I thought was a Secret Service guy hiding on the roof. Do they stay there all night, or can they come down at night then go back up the next morning?

Anyway, those are some of the questions I had about life in the white house. I hope I didn't bother you with this, as I guess you have a lot more important things to do than answer dumb questions from some hick in the middle of nowhere (like me). Good luck, Sir, in your coming four years.

Yours,

K. Burridge (age: 66)

THE WHITE HOUSE

WASHINGTON

October 22, 2012

Dear Mr. Burridge:

Thanks so much for your interesting letter and questions about life in the White House. When I have time, I like reading 'National Geographic' as well. The White House was designed by James Hoban, and built between 1792 and 1800 of white-painted Aquia Creek sandstone in the Neoclassical style. Please drop in and visit us on your next trip to Washington. If I'm home then, perhaps I can show you around.

Sincerely,

Barack Obama

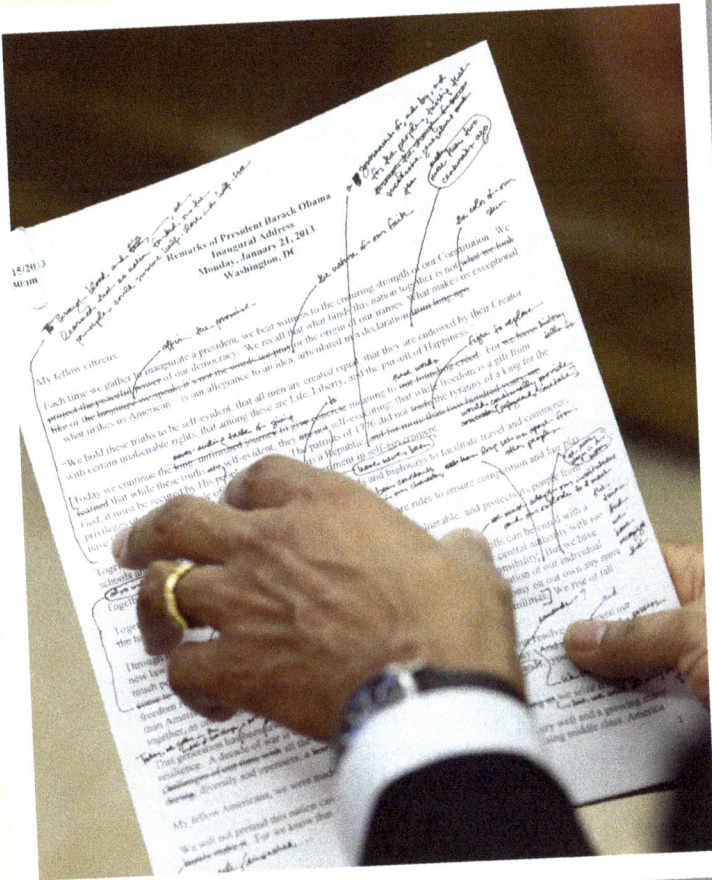

President Obama corrects his daughter
Malia's homework assignment during
a quiet evening at home.

LOCKHEED MARTIN

January 15, 2013

Dear Mr. President:

On behalf of the entire Lockheed
Martin family, I would like to be one
of the first to congratulate you on
your stunning re-election victory in
November. We are confident that the
country will, once again, be in
extremely capable hands over the
course of the next four years.

As you very well know, Lockheed Martin
is at the forefront of providing
America with the most technologically
advanced fighter aircraft available in
the world today. Employing over
123,000 people across the globe, and
118,000 domestically, LM is one of the
largest, most reliable, and most
experienced defense contractors the
world has ever known.

Everyone at LM is especially proud
that LM was chosen to build and supply
the F-35 Lightning II fighter aircraft
to the U.S. Government for its defense
needs. In case you don't already know
due to your extremely hectic schedule,
the L-35 is a family of single-seat,
single-engine, fifth generation
multirole fighters, used to perform
ground attack, reconnaissance, and air
defense missions with stealth

capability. It carried out its first
successful flight on 15 December 2006.

The United States is contracted to
purchase a total of 2,443 of these
aircraft, which, when finally
operational, will be used to provide
tactical airpower for the U.S. Air
Force, Marine Corps and Navy during
the coming decade.

As you no doubt have probably already
heard from Secretary Panetta, the GAO
warned that excessive design testing
and retrofitting of the J-35 could
lead to extensive cost overruns,
forcing us to re-price the entire
system. In February 2011, the Pentagon
put an original price of $207.6
million on each of the 32 aircraft to
be acquired in 2012. Regrettably, Sir,
I have to inform you that this figure
will most likely rise to at least
$304.15 million per aircraft sometime
in the near future. As a result, if
the entire order of 2,433 J-35
aircraft are taken for delivery by the
Pentagon, the additional cost will be
approximately $237 billion.

Mr. President, when Lockheed Martin
accepted the profound responsibility
of taking on the J-35 program, which
you may or may not know arose out of a
private ski weekend and subsequent
meeting I had with Vice President
Cheney at the Jackson Hole Defense
Conclave in 2005, it was our original
intent to deliver these aircraft on
budget and on time. Although we have
for the most part kept up our end of
the bargain, there is no hiding the
fact that the program is now seriously

behind schedule, as well as somewhat over budget.

Please rest assured, Mr. President, that everyone in the LM family is working diligently, day and night, to repair the various small hiccups that have occurred while building this great and worthwhile aircraft. It is our firm and confident belief that the trust America placed in Lockheed Martin at the outset was not misplaced, and that this trust will not go un-returned.

Thank you.

Sincerely,

Byron C. Hedgers III, COO

LOCKHEED MARTIN CO.

Bethesda, MD

April 16, 2011

Dear Mr. President O'Bama:

Recently, I've been lisning to your great speeches about how in American anyone can grow up to be anything they want as long as they work hard and stay out of prison. My father told me that was all a bunch of "liberal crap", but deep in my heart I believe it too (not that it's a bunch of crap but you can get ahead if you work hard and stay out of jail.)

Right now I'm in the eleventh grade at the Truman High School. I had to repeat eleventh grade three times because that darn fool Ms. Goolsby woodn't pass me in remedial english. But when she does I'm gonna go to the local community college, then from there...well, I know this sounds crazy, but I'm gonna try for medical school.

See, as long as I can remember, (and that's not my strong suit), I've always wanted to be a thoracic surgeon. I don't know what thoracic means, 'cept I heard my buddy Earl talking about how his father needed a good one back six years ago when he worked at the sewage treetment plant. His dad died anyway, but from that time on I always had this idea of becoming a thoracic surgeon, and maybe helping poor kids in Apachalia or Detroit or some other godforsaken place and at the same time make tons of money, which of course I'd give all to charity.

So, is there anyway you or the Secret Service could contact Ms. Goolsby here at the school (address below) and tell her to pass me so I can get the hell out of here (like tomorrow) and become a doctor? If she says no at first, you may have to try a few more times because she's ornery as hell and stubborn as a g.d. mule.

Sincerely,

Chester Lumpkin

Truman Regional High School

422 Budworth Ave.

Coffeeville, KS   67337

THE WHITE HOUSE

WASHINGTON

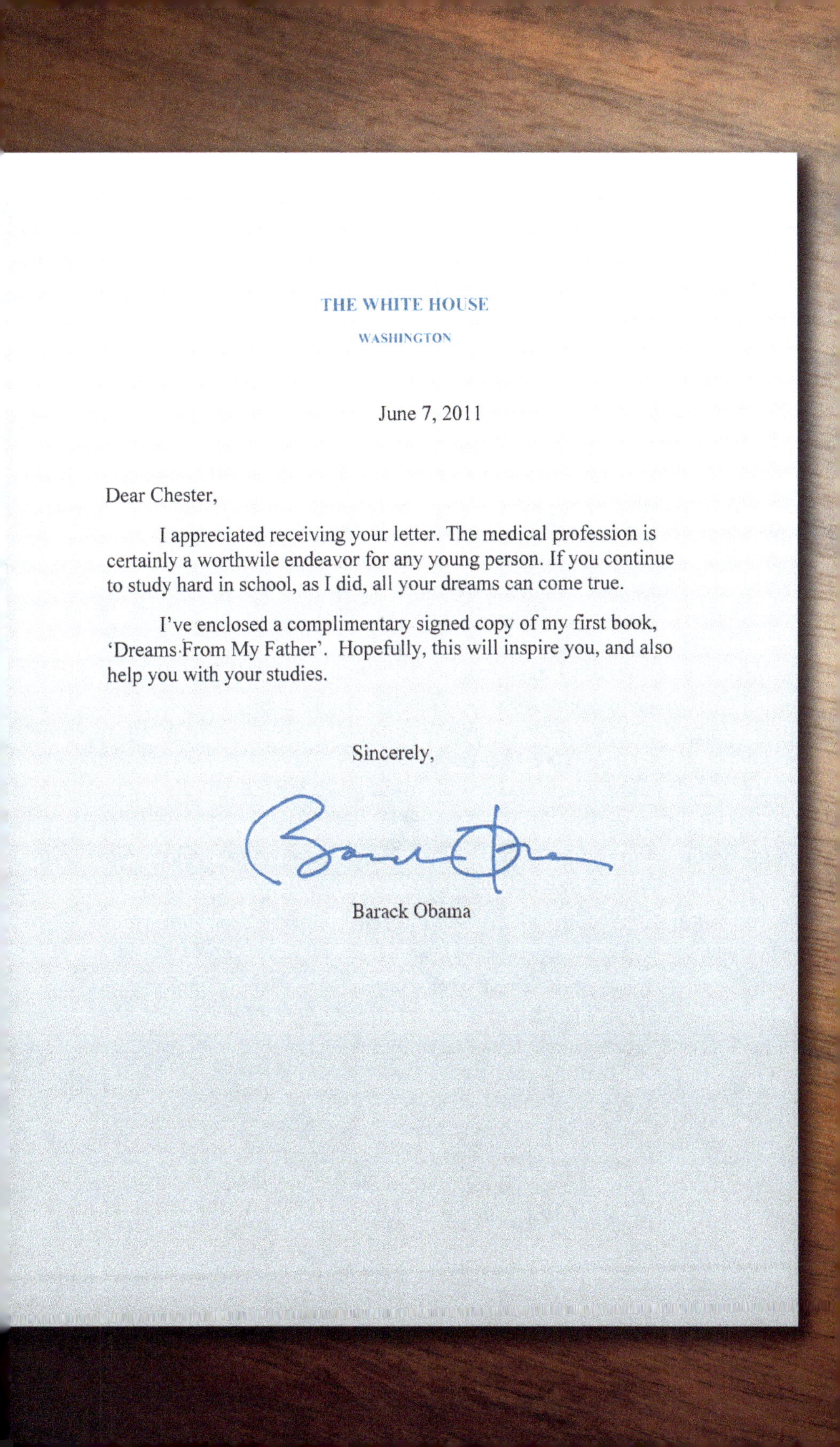

June 7, 2011

Dear Chester,

I appreciated receiving your letter. The medical profession is certainly a worthwile endeavor for any young person. If you continue to study hard in school, as I did, all your dreams can come true.

I've enclosed a complimentary signed copy of my first book, 'Dreams From My Father'. Hopefully, this will inspire you, and also help you with your studies.

Sincerely,

Barack Obama

Feb. 19, 2013

Dear Mrs. Obama:

I am writing to you today to thank you for being such a great First Lady, and for looking so ravishing and lovely at the White House events I watched recently on TV. Every time I see you, I'm proud to be an American, proud I voted for your husband, and just generally proud to be living in the greatest country on Earth!

I totally disagree with some TV reporters who said your dress was "too flouncy." The "Victory" red color was perfect, as well. I think I saw sort of the same thing at Wal-Mart the other day, and when I can afford it I might go back and purchase it for my cousin's wedding in July. (And after I lose forty pounds!)

But, I have a personal question. Is the president, Barack, neat and thoughtful? I mean, does he pick up his clothes at night, or does he leave them strewn all over the Lincoln bedroom floor, like mine does? Because of the bad economy, I work three jobs right now, and get home around two in the morning after an hour's drive home from the hospital where I work as a nurse's assistant. By that time, my husband Gibb's been home for five or six hours already (he drives a school bus). When I get home I find not only the kitchen's a total disaster, with beer and f---ing wine bottles plus a pile of g.d. leftovers and empty pizza boxes strewn all over the place, but when I go into the bedroom his clothes are all over the floor, his (dirty) underwear is hanging from the bedpost, and, well, it's like a nuclear bomb hit the place. I swear, if he keeps it up it might be time to dig out the old 12-guage and let him have it!

Also, does your husband brush his teeth three times a day, or because of his hectic schedule only occasionally? Again, I ask because Gibb brushes <u>at most</u> once every three days, and as a result he can come on stronger than a g.d. garbage truck. The stink is almost too much to bear sometimes.

I love my husband, and I think he loves me too. But is there any advice you can give to someone who's at her breaking point?

Sincerely,

Trudy A. Ebersol

Plentywood, Montana

Dear President Obama,

My name's Billy Osgood. I am in Miss Hunter's fourth grade class. She assigned us to write a letter to someone we respect, so I chose you.

We live in a big white house too. My Dad didn't unnerstand why I chose you because he said you were a "stooge of the left wing," whatever that means. But I like you, especially when you play basketball and give speeches (but not long ones), so here goes.

My question is how come your hair is getting grey when at first it was all black? My Mom says itz because you have to talk with lots of difficult people in Washington, like senators and congressmen and members of the "Izreel lobby", whatever that is. She says you also have to deal with "whiners" (like poor &

homeless people all across America, not just in your own town.

Are they right, or is it something else like the White House is too hot or you don't eat enuff?

I play second base in Little League, and this afternoon we're going to play this team that's not nice. Sometimes wen they lose they throw stuff at us. My Mom says itz because the kids making trouble are probably either african-american or "ill eagle", whatever that means. Miss Hunter says itz because they don't eat well so they get angry easily. I don't know who's rite, but when I grow up I want to be a sicologist so I can study people and figure out why they're so messed up, like these kids we're playing.

Anyway, my hand's tired from riting, so I'll quit and go out and play with Mike, my best friend who's father is in prison for "incider trading & wire frawd", whatever those are.

Sincerely,

Billy Osgood, Miss Hunter's fourth Grade

President Obama patiently models a new sweater for *Vogue Magazine*.

October 20, 2012

Dear President Obama:

As President of Ohioans for Obama, I would like to thank you for all you've done, not only for our beloved country, but also for Ohio, the 'Mother of Presidents'. As the mother of five children myself, I'm confident you'll be re-elected in November to another term. Also, I'm a president too, so I know what it feels like to run for high elective office (ha, ha).

At this stage in the campaign, I would guess you're pretty nervous about the outcome. To calm your nerves a little, as I was folding the laundry the other day I came up with a list of reasons why you'll win the election:

- Ohio begins with the letter O, as does "Obama".
- You already won Ohio once in '08 – you'll do it again. And this time you're up against Romney, who got three military deferments, unlike Sen. McCain who was a war hero!

- When I was at the Ohio State Fair in July, I heard many negative remarks by the people there (especially at the 4-H shed) about Governor Romney, like he hated poor people and had all these homes he never even uses.

- Chicago, your home town, isn't that far from us. My husband Greg works in sales and drives there all the time and loves it, even though it's windy and cold as the dickens.

- My grandmother Bessie is 98 years old, and has always voted for the winner of the presidential election. She said she'll vote for you once again this time, too. (I'll be driving her from the nursing home to the polls. Sorry, my granddad, who's 99, is a Republican and thinks you're a "commie socialist". We love him anyway.)

- The kids at my son Sean's school, Bruning Elementary, took a straw poll and they elected you by sixteen votes. Like my grandma Bessie, they've never been wrong.

Those are just some of the reasons why you shouldn't worry. Please do the best you can, and give our love to your beautiful wife, Michelle, as well as your beautiful children who must fill you with boundless pride and joy, as our kids do, every day.

Stacey-Ann Zwicker, President

Ohioans for Obama

OHIOANS FOR OHIO

July 4, 2012

Dear President Obama:

On behalf of all the citizens of our great state, I would like to thank you for your recent visits to Ohio, "The Buckeye State" and "Mother of Presidents".

As you very well know, every four years Ohio regains the spotlight for its importance in our national elections. Regrettably, very few of the presidential contenders who visit with us stop to ponder one very important fact: if Ohio didn't exist, there'd be a giant black gap between Pennsylvania and Indiana.

For your edification, below is a list of other little-known facts about the 17th State:

• The official state rock song is "Hang On Sloopy".

•Ohio is the leading producer of nursery & greenhouse plants.

•Ohio has an area of 116,103 sq. miles. It ranks 34th in state size.

•Ohio is the only state where its state flag is of a pennant design.

•The following personalities are from Ohio: Steven Spielberg, Drew Carey, Annie Oakley, Paul Newman, Arsenio Hall, Clark Gable, Charles Manson, and Jeffrey Dahmer.

• Founded in 1788 by General Rufus Putnam, Marietta - named after the then Queen of France Marie Antoinette - was Ohio's first permanent settlement.

•Columbus is Ohio's state capital (even though Chillicothe was the 1st) & largest city.

•Half of the US population lives within a 500 mile radius of the city of Columbus.

•In 1899, the first full time automobile service station was opened in Ohio.

•The automobile self-starter was invented by Charles Kettering of Loudonville in 1911.

•Teflon was invented by Roy J. Plunkett of New Carlisle in 1938.

•The world's largest basket is located in Dresden Ohio at Basket Village USA.

•On the north side of Kelleys Island in Ohio, The Glacial Grooves on the north side of Kelleys Island - scoured into solid limestone bedrock about 18,000 years ago by the great ice sheet - are the largest easily accessible glacial grooves in the world.

•Fostoria is the only city in Ohio that is situated in 3 counties (Hancock, Seneca & Wood).

•A famous earthen mound in the shape of a serpent near Peebles Ohio, Serpent Mound State Memorial, winds along for a total length of 411 m (1348 ft.).

• The United States Public Land Survey Ordinance of 1785 - providing the administration and subdivision of land in the Old Northwest Territory, was first enacted from the starting point of East Liverpool in Ohio. From this starting point, this rectangular-grid land survey divided all public lands into townships six mile squares.

•Cincinnati was the home of the first professional city fire department.

•The Y Bridge in Zanesville Ohio, built in 1814, spanning the confluence of the Licking and Muskingum Rivers, is one of the most unique bridges in the world. Deemed by "Ripley's Believe It or Not" as the only bridge where you can cross and still be on the same side of the river.

•As a solution to halting the pilfering of his profits by patrons, James J. Ritty, of Dayton Ohio, invented the cash register in 1879.

•La Rue, Ohio was the home of the first gasoline powered fire engine.

•In 1891, John Lambert of Ohio City made America's first automobile, though was unable to sell one.

•Ohio Automobile Company (later to be called the Packard Motor Car Company) was founded in Warren Ohio in 1900, to compete with the product manufactured by The Winton Motor Carriage Company.

•In 2008, Cleveland ranked 7th as the most dangerous city in the US among cities with a population of 100,000 to 500,000 and the 11th most dangerous overall.

I hope the above was helpful to you, and that it will help you gain a deeper appreciation of Ohio's history, and its people.

Good luck with the campaign, and we look forward to seeing you out here in our neighborhood again soon!

Sincerely,

Homer Brindall

Homer Brindall, Executive V.P.

Ohioans for Ohio

THE WHITE HOUSE

WASHINGTON

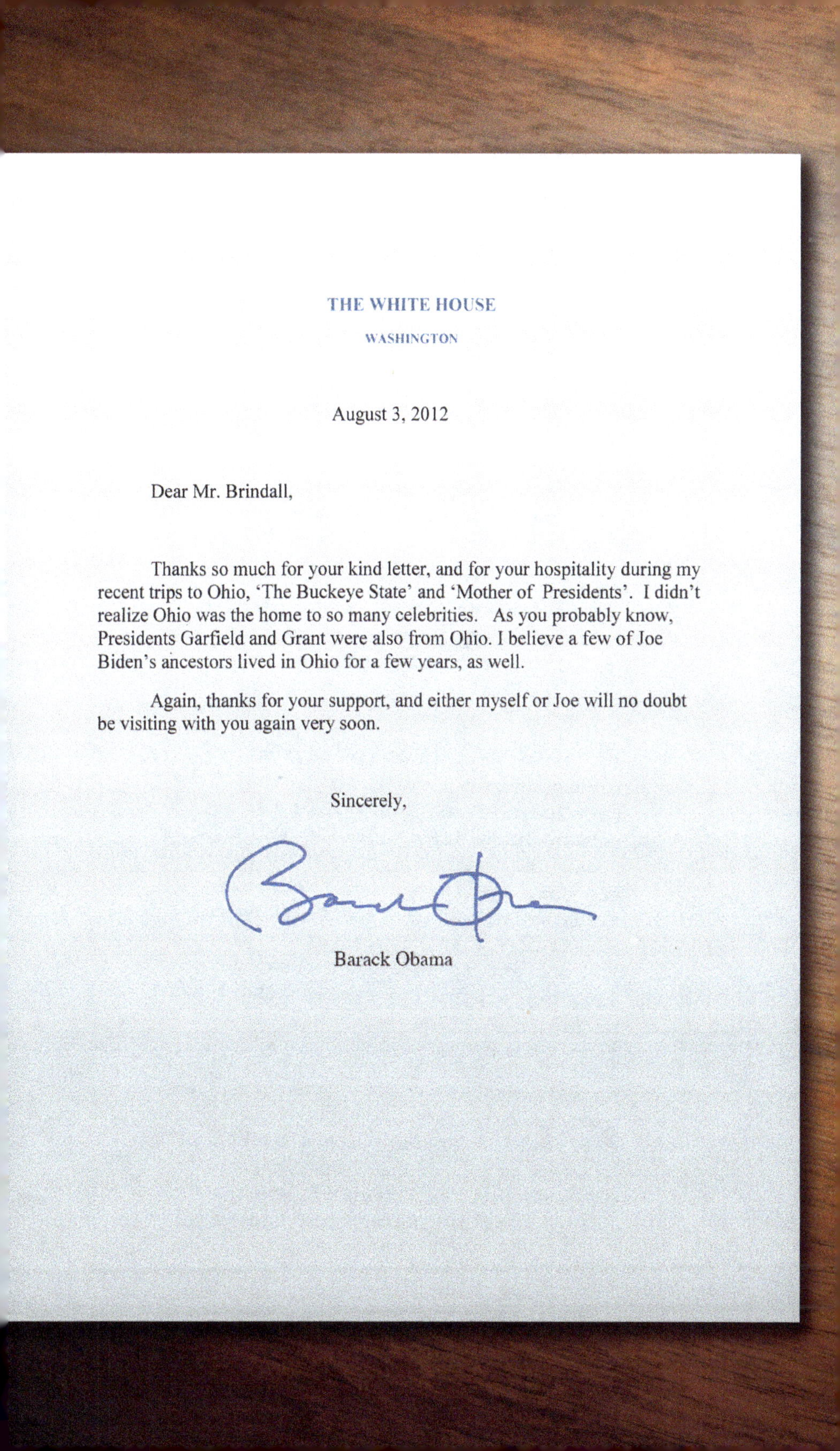

August 3, 2012

Dear Mr. Brindall,

Thanks so much for your kind letter, and for your hospitality during my recent trips to Ohio, 'The Buckeye State' and 'Mother of Presidents'. I didn't realize Ohio was the home to so many celebrities. As you probably know, Presidents Garfield and Grant were also from Ohio. I believe a few of Joe Biden's ancestors lived in Ohio for a few years, as well.

Again, thanks for your support, and either myself or Joe will no doubt be visiting with you again very soon.

Sincerely,

Barack Obama

August 16, 2012

Dear President Obama:

My name is Phoebe Denkler. Currently,
I'm a waitress at Lou's Café here in
downtown Smudge, OK.

Even though I've been a hard worker
and have never missed a day of work
for any reason in over 36 years on the
job, I was recently informed by
certified mail that my hours are being
cut from 72 to 43.

Mr. President, in these days of
recession and high unemployment, it's
very hard if not impossible for a
person of my ilk to make a go of it if
I can only work 43 hours. My wages
are only $ 5.18 per hour to begin
with, which were raised three years
ago from $ 4.83 but are still pretty
low and getting nearly impossible to
live on, especially considering I have
to drive 83 miles (each way) to get
from my home to work.

To make matters a lot worse, my
brother Zell just returned from
overseas (S. Korea) with a bashed left
hand he got in a bar brawl there, so
he can't help me. Even if he wasn't
injured, he's lazy as hell and he's

already taken to hanging out down by
The Silo (that's a bar here in town)
with that tramp Laverne.

So, my question is this: is there
anything, anything at all you can do
to help the economic climate here in
Oklahoma, because if you could then
maybe they could give me more hours at
the café and I could pay the rent on
my studio apartment and help my
brother.

Mr. President, we live in a truly
great country, which each day I give
thanks to the Lord I'm a citizen of.
But with this economy the way it is,
there's just so much a person can
endure before that person has to do
something really drastic…

       Yours truly,

       Phoebe Deckler

       (Smudge, OK)

President Obama aboard R.M.S. Titanic just prior to hitting an iceberg in the North Atlantic.

June 26, 2010

Dear Mr. President Obama,

My name is Eb Billings. You don't know me and most likely never heard of me and most likely never will. That's because I keep quiet and generally mind my own business, unlike a lot of other people in this country who always feel they have to complain or march through the street or otherwise make a ruckus about something. Like those young whippersnappers that riled the country last year with their anti-Wall Street slogans and by putting up tents in the middle of traffic to protest something or other which I was never able to make sense of due to the fact that it probably made no sense in the first place, at least not to me, and probably to 99 per cent of the rest of the folks in our blessed country who're too busy making a living or just getting to work or putting food on the table or bringing up their kinfolk to worry about it much. As for myself, I'll just stay here on my porch in my rocking chair, as I have for the past 23 years since I retired, and keep my problems to myself, even though I got a ton of 'em like my bursitis and this darned ringing in both ears which my doctor says is from the war injury I picked up in Korea, although it could've been from that semi which hit me on the interstate during that storm back in '58. But who cares? The main thing is, each man has to do what's right for himself, and for me that means watching the traffic go by and going to church every Sunday and doing unto others and all what the good Lord above expects us to without complaining about it, like those ungrateful whippersnappers I mentioned before. But I'm sort of getting off track here and away from my main point which is that I'm just one old man sitting in an old rocking chair in West Virginia minding his own business while every day of every year every dang blasted person you meet seems to have something he has to get off his chest. But I've run on way too long myself, so I'll stop yammering and get back to my carving. If you think I've said too much, well, you wouldn't be the first. The wife says I talk too much too, once I get going. Anyways, good luck to you, and don't forget to say your prayers.

Eb Billings

Flatwoods, West Virginia

PILTREE PLUMBING & HEATING CO. INC.

November 27, 2012

Dear President Obama,

Thanks so much for your recent visit to
Piltree Plumbing & Heating Company. Our
small staff was overjoyed by your visit to
us in October, not only to our showroom but
to the entire southern Ohio area. Ohio, The
Mother of Presidents, was glad to have you!

As I told you during your far too brief
stop, our customers have told us time and
time again how much they value how quickly
and thoroughly Piltree Plumbing and Heating
works to service all their plumbing needs,
large and small.

From a faucet that won't stop leaking to
clogged drains, cracked pipes, no hot
water, and so much more, Piltree Plumbing
provides professional plumbing repairs
throughout the greater Dayton area. (We
also serve Kettering and Xenia.)

Now that you've been re-elected, Mr.
President, I guess we won't be seeing you
that regularly in Ohio any more. Should you
see fit to visit us again, however, <u>please</u>
try to schedule us for more than the 2 ½
minutes you gave us the first time. And
please also try to bring Michelle along --
we'd love to see her, too. (We have some
great new shower and bathroom fixtures I
think she'd be very interested in,
including the new Sani-Flush by Broadmoor.)

Yours sincerely,

Ed Piltree, Jr.

PILTREE PLUMBING & HEATING

Member, Southern Ohio Better Heating
Council

Member, Dayton Chamber of Commerce

September 23rd, 2008

Dear Mrs. Obama,

My name is Tammy Johnson and I live in Johnsonville, Minnesota. I am writing to say how happy and proud I am you are the First Lady of our country, and to congratulate you on being declared the winner of the Family Circle Presidential Cookie Bake-Off. Your white and dark chocolate-chip cookies defeated the M&M cookies submitted by Republican rival Ann Romney, and deservedly so.

Seeing you every day on TV, you look so proud when you're with your husband and two beautiful children. They must be a great source of pride for both of you, as our six children are for me and my husband, John.

We're especially proud of our eldest son, John, Jr., who recently returned from his seventh tour in Afghanistan. John Jr. was a somewhat troubled young man, always gravitating toward the wrong crowd and getting into scrapes. Fortunately, he buckled down eventually and grew into a strapping 18-year-old eager to enlist in the Army and proudly serve our proud country.

Although John Junior is wonderful and makes all of us in the extended Johnson clan full of pride, we're also very proud of his younger brother Johnny, our fifteen year old, who was just named co-captain of the junior varsity football team. Johnny is the spitting image of his father, whose extreme pridefulness can be seen each time Johnny proudly runs down the field for a touchdown or completes a long pass. We're also highly proud (although not as proud as we are with Johnny and John Jr.) of our only daughter, Jennie, who after struggling academically in high school, just recently enrolled in secretarial school in nearby East Johnsonville.

We're also profoundly proud of our sixteen grand kids, who luckily live close by and are always coming over for family get-togethers and celebrations whenever there's anything to celebrate or be prideful about.

Well, that's about all I wanted to say. Please say hello to your husband, the President, and keep giving us great cookie recipes which we can treasure forever.

Sincerely,

Tammy Johnson

President Obama stabs himself in the forehead while reading a memo from Hilary Clinton.

February 23, 2010

Dear President Obama:

I'm typing this letter to you by candlelight in order to save money for my family which, like many families across the country, is hurting in the current economic downturn.

My husband Steve and I have six children. Steve recently lost his job as a greeter at Wal-Mart, and even with my job as a file clerk, things have gotten pretty dire for us financially.

On the positive side, it's amazing the ideas you can come up with when you're forced to save money. In the last couple of months, we've discovered some tricks almost any family can use to save hard-earned cash. Here's a few of them:

1. I have to drive 162 miles (each way) to get to my job. I save a little by walking the last five miles when I finally get there. I estimate we save 52 cents a day, which can add up.
2. Because of all the break-ins in our neighborhood, we used to have a security system for our small home. To save money, we installed an electrified six-foot-high perimeter fence. The extra amperage is more than made up for by the savings.
3. Because of budget cutbacks, in July our town closed its fire department. To make up for it, we now keep a five-gallon bucket of water in every room.
4. We were spending over $4,000 each winter on heating bills. We save big now by only heating the TV room; we spend 95% of our time there,

and when we're asleep in the bedroom we don't feel the cold anyway.

5. When he goes duck hunting with his pals, instead of filling his pickup with a full 20 gallons, (which costs $85), my husband puts in only 19 gallons. This saves him $4.25, which he can then use for a few extra rounds of ammunition.

6. Six children are expensive to feed, so each day the kids pick straws and the loser doesn't get dinner. (This not only saves valuable pennies, but it's also fun for the kids, as well!)

7. Finally: We now cook everything using fresh-cut firewood. Carbon monoxide can be a silent killer, so we installed CO alarms my parents gave us throughout the house.

Anyway, Mr. President, that's just a very small sampling of how the Truesdales are saving during this Great Recession we're now in. Hopefully, this advice will be helpful to other struggling families like us, all across America.

Sincerely Yours,

Barb Truesdale

Glendo, Wyoming

AMBLIN
ENTERTAINMENT

January 25, 2013

Dear Mr. President,

Congratulations on your re-election victory! It was great seeing you, Michelle, and the kids at the inaugural ball last weekend. I hope you had as wonderful and exciting a time as I did.

You asked during our brief chat in Washington if I thought your life and presidency so far would make an interesting, compelling film, and whether I might entertain the idea of producing such a film. My answer, emphatically, is 'yes' to both questions.

The film I envision would open on the dusty hillsides of western Kenya. It's here that your paternal grandfather, Hussein, worked as a cook and herbalist. Hussein Obama could be played by the great Oscar-winning actor Morgan Freeman (*The Bucket List, Conan the Barbarian*) whose calm voice and authoritarian manner would echo the various struggles your ancestors made to survive and endure with dignity.

We quickly bring your story up to modern times, where your father, Barack Sr., a highly intelligent, honest man, is working as an economist for the Kenyan government. After some thought, I realized Samuel L. Jackson (*Pulp Fiction, Snakes on a Plane*) who's not only a fine leading actor but who's also able to play bad guys and drug dealers, would be a perfect fit as your father (assuming Quentin Tarantino has no plans for him which might interfere).

As "Obama" proceeds quickly toward the present day, the film shows you as a young man growing up in Kansas, where you're being reared by your grandparents now that your mother has moved back to Indonesia. For the role of your maternal grandmother "Toot" Dunham, I'd like to suggest Sally Field (*Lincoln, The Flying Nun*), or perhaps Tippi Hedren (*The Birds*), both of whom always bring gravitas mixed with a dollop of humor to any role. I think your mother, Stanley, should be played by Meryl Streep (*The Iron Lady, The Ant Bully*), an Oscar-winning performer who many consider to be our greatest living actress.

While Will Smith (who like you is of mixed African-American and Native-American heritage) is a slam dunk for you as president, I see the part of your recent Defense Secretary, Leon Panetta, being played with gusto by either Al Pacino (*Scarface, Scent of a Woman*), or by Bobby DeNiro (*Taxi Driver, The King of Comedy*), who along with

Meryl would no doubt help make the film a serious contender come Oscar time.

Finally, the part of Michelle, your beautiful, lovely, gifted wife and mother to your two gorgeous gifted children, must be depicted by an actress of sterling abilities and great sensitivity. Again, after some thought, I realized Whoopi Goldberg (*The Color Purple*, *Late Night With Jimmy Fallon*) would be the perfect choice. Whoopi, (nee Caryn Elaine Johnson) not only has a long resume, but she's also usually available. I'm confident she'd be more than eager to take on the challenges of such a role.

Your years in the White House provide many opportunities not only for poignant drama but also numerous action scenes, which I see occurring in the desolate wastes of Iraq and Afghanistan as our brave soldiers fight the evil Taliban hordes. These scenes, showing in great and bloody detail the chaotic mayhem which accompanies the horrors of war, could be shot either at the Universal Studios lot, or at Death Valley, California, both of which are clearly more economical than moving an entire U.S. Army brigade back overseas.

There's literally thousands of writers we could hire to execute the story and screenplay, but, quite frankly, I haven't given this part of the equation much thought yet.

My back-of-the-hand estimate is that this film could be shot on a 450-day schedule with a budget of around 400 million dollars. If we rolled the film out in 4200 theaters just before you leave office, my expectation is that total (domestic) box office revenues could be as much as 750 million dollars, depending on which actors are eventually used, as well as the weather the opening weekend.

All in all, I feel extremely confident we could make a great film that's not only worthwhile for its historical value (*Lincoln, Saving Private Ryan*) but also for its dramatic and action potential (*Jaws, Sugarland Express*).

Assuming my calendar is clear and that our representatives are able to construct a deal which is satisfactory to both of us, I'd be proud to not only to produce this film, but also to direct it.

I eagerly await your input on all of this.

In the meantime, stay well and good luck in your second term!

All the best,

Steven Spielberg

SS/df

THE WHITE HOUSE

WASHINGTON

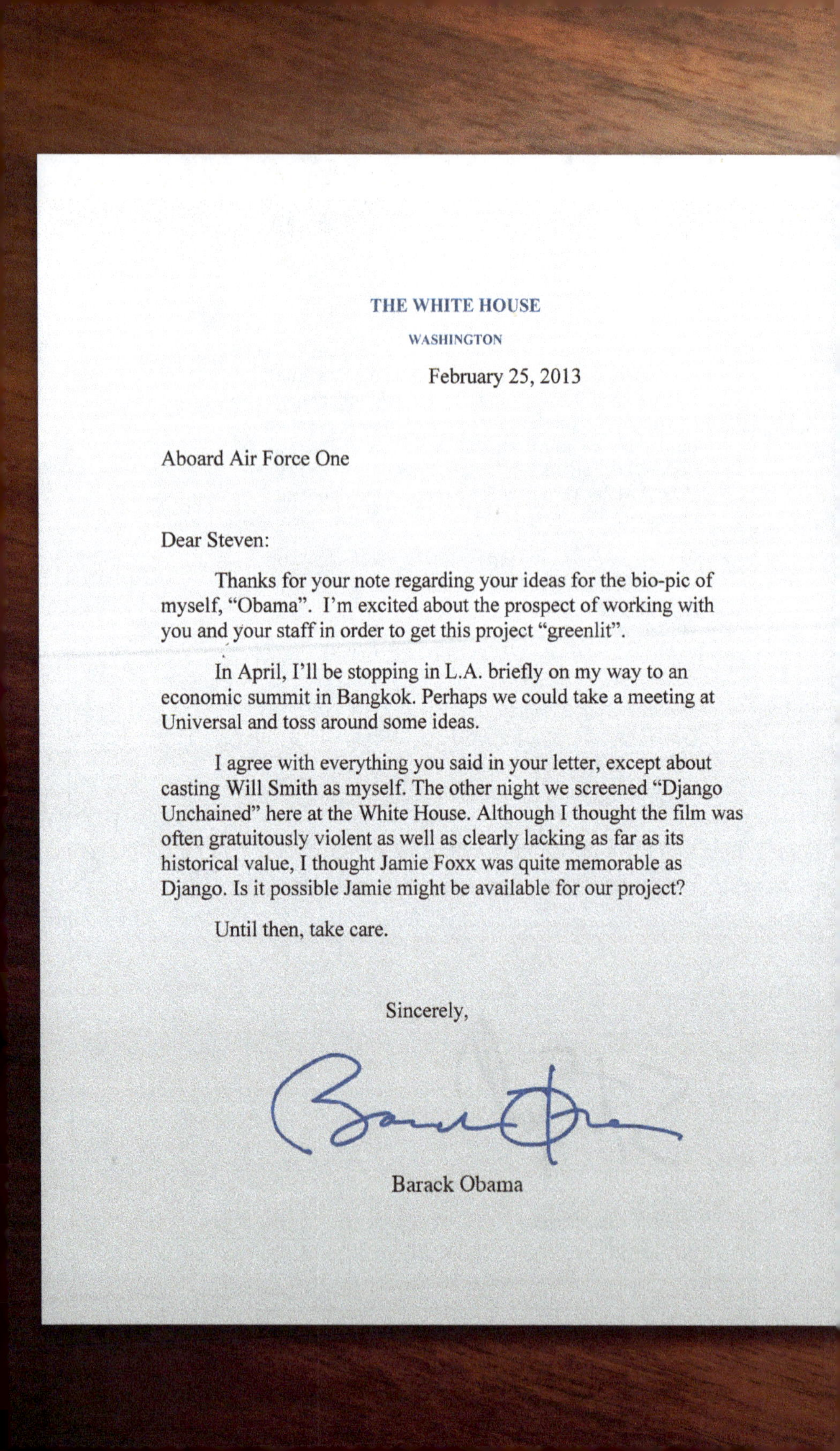

February 25, 2013

Aboard Air Force One

Dear Steven:

Thanks for your note regarding your ideas for the bio-pic of myself, “Obama”. I’m excited about the prospect of working with you and your staff in order to get this project “greenlit”.

In April, I’ll be stopping in L.A. briefly on my way to an economic summit in Bangkok. Perhaps we could take a meeting at Universal and toss around some ideas.

I agree with everything you said in your letter, except about casting Will Smith as myself. The other night we screened “Django Unchained” here at the White House. Although I thought the film was often gratuitously violent as well as clearly lacking as far as its historical value, I thought Jamie Foxx was quite memorable as Django. Is it possible Jamie might be available for our project?

Until then, take care.

Sincerely,

Barack Obama

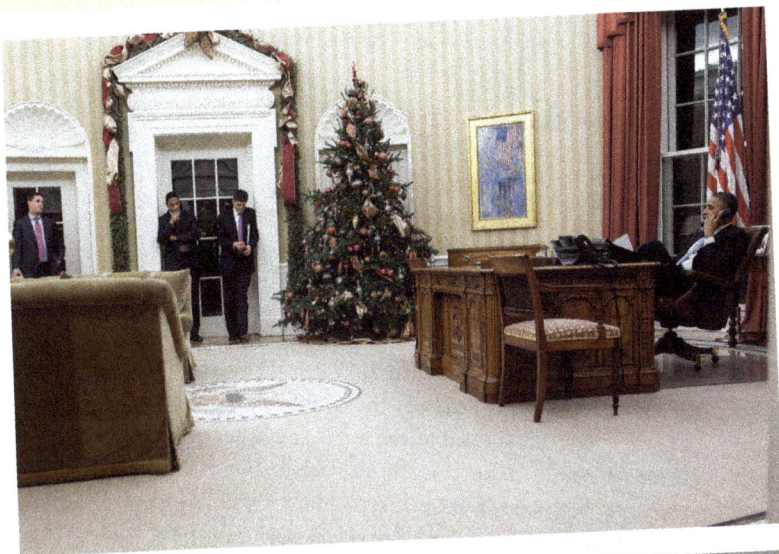

President Obama telephones
Santa Claus from the Oval Office.

June 20, 2012

Dear President Obama,

I realize you're extremely busy with the 2012 campaign, but I wanted to write to you regarding the problems this country is currently having with student debt, which you mentioned in a recent speech while visiting Ohio.

Last May, I graduated from Veneer University in Capon, Illinois. Because my family isn't rich (they could probably be described as lower middle class), I was forced to take out a large number of student loans to pay my way through school. Although after six years of both study and working part time in the university laundry I was finally awarded a diploma in small business marketing, I suddenly found myself buried under a mountain of debt, to the extent that I now owe a total of $897,344.33. This money is owed to 17 different banks, but mostly to CBL Educational Loans of Buford, Illinois.

Mr. President, I never imagined when I enrolled at Veneer that I would eventually owe this kind of money upon graduation. Like most eighteen year olds desperate to attend college, I simply signed an unintelligible stack of paperwork without looking closely at the words. Although this was mostly my own fault, it's also partly the fault of the banks that preyed on my vulnerability as a young person willing to do almost anything to gain a foothold in the middle class.

At the current rate of repayment from my job as an assistant custodian at a Moline elementary school, it will take me approximately 147.4 years to pay back this loan in full, assuming I live that long which is doubtful considering I'm working almost 60 hours a week, with no benefits like health insurance or paid vacation time.

If you're fortunate enough to be re-elected, Sir, I urge you to work with Congress to enact some kind of legislation which will allow me to get out of these loans and start putting money away for a nice home in the suburbs and, eventually, a comfortable retirement. Congress will obviously not do anything alone, so you must, any way you can!

Sincerely,

Tim Terwilliger

Moline, Illinois

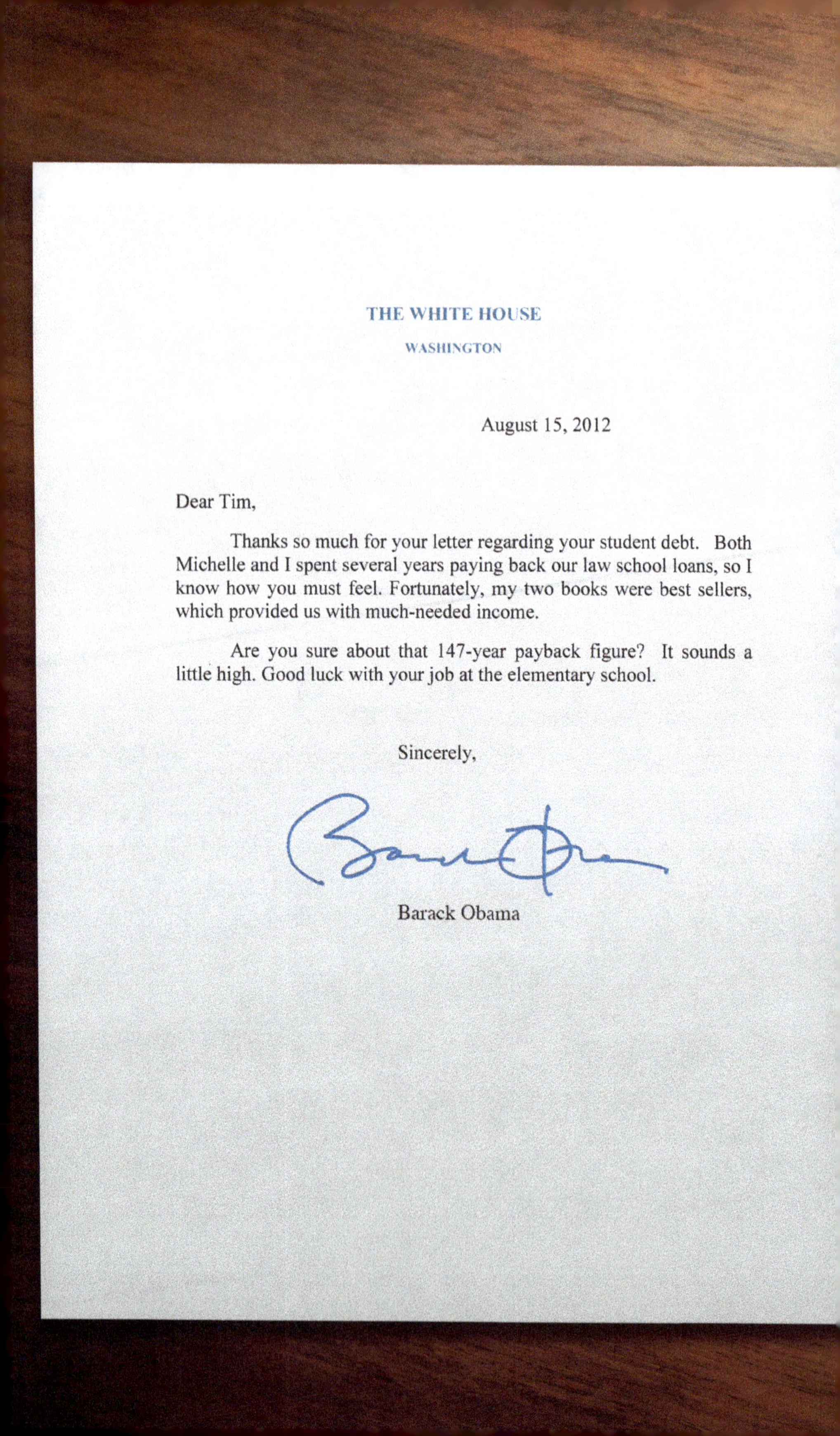

THE WHITE HOUSE

WASHINGTON

August 15, 2012

Dear Tim,

Thanks so much for your letter regarding your student debt. Both Michelle and I spent several years paying back our law school loans, so I know how you must feel. Fortunately, my two books were best sellers, which provided us with much-needed income.

Are you sure about that 147-year payback figure? It sounds a little high. Good luck with your job at the elementary school.

Sincerely,

Barack Obama

Some letters to the President are typed and some are handwritten. Most, however, are written in crayon and are barely legible.

November 24, 2011

Dear President Obama:

When I was a youngster, I dreamed
of one day becoming president of
the United States, like you.

Instead, my path in life took me
to where I am now, a senior
accountant in the firm of Ogilvy,
Taft, Hunter and Gray.

Each day for the last twenty six
years, I've sat in a fluorescent-
lit air-conditioned office here
on the 37th floor of the Heard
Building, hunched over reams of
agonizingly dull spreadsheets and
expense reports, trying to figure
out how to save some filthy rich
retiree in Grosse Pointe a couple
of bucks on his personal tax
returns.

My days can be characterized by
utter drudgery, my nights a
numbingly tedious 29-year
marriage to a woman I should

never have married, WHO IS ALSO
AN ACCOUNTANT.

You made your dream come true.
For me and all other Americans
like me, stay true to yourself
and do what's best for our great
country. We're counting on you.

    Sincerely,

    Edward Byfield

March 8, 2013

Dear President Obama:

I would've congratulated you on your victory back in November, which was probably the result of some kind of fraud, but I can't because I'm a Republican and I didn't vote for you. There are hundreds of reasons why I'd never vote for you, but the main one is simple: The 2nd Amendment to our beloved Constitution.

As a longtime card-carrying member of the NRA (National Rifle Assoc.), I can confidently state that you are typical of all the leftist pansies and homo-lovers in this country who would rather destroy our liberties and freedoms, in other words our whole American way of life, than allow even one person to carry a firearm, which is clearly our God-given right.

You say you enjoy skeet shooting and are in favor of the rights of citizens like myself to bear arms, but your actions don't match your words. Anytime there's a so-called "massacre" in this country, you say guns must be curtailed. But why? Thirty-nine thousand people are killed each year in traffic accidents. Does that mean we should get rid of all our cars? (How would I get to the gun shop?) Each year there's 500,000 cancer deaths. Does that mean we should outlaw smoking, also a God-given right and which has helped my family earn a living for the last 200 years?

Sir, you do not deserve a second term because you have not upheld the solemn oath you took the first time, which is to abide by the constitution and allow anyone that can breathe to carry a gun, the bigger the better. (Me and my wife

Patty own sixteen shotguns, 7 AR-15's, an anti-tank gun, an RPG launcher, thirty two pistols, and 25,000 rounds of ammunition, all of which are perfectly legal, or should be, here in Tennessee.)

Sir, I believe every American living in this country (legally) should be allowed to carry an unlicensed weapon OF ANY KIND into ANY SCHOOL OR PUBLIC BUILDING he or she wants to so long as no innocent little children are threatened. If you disagree with that, then as president you should resign immediately.

Yours truly,

Clayton Ebbers, Jr.

Dixon, Tennessee

July 3, 2010

Dear President Obama,

This letter is just to thank you so very much for deciding to run for president for a second time.

My family loves watching you as you battle all those mean old men down the street in Congress, especially that evil John Boehner who if you ask me looks like a shifty car salesman. I wouldn't trust him with a dollar bill let alone our whole economy!

The main thing, though, and why I'm glad you ran again, is that you have such a beautiful family. Michelle is always stunning. She has a beautiful face and a great smile, and she's so smart! (She went to Harvard too, right?) And your kids, Sasha and Malia, they're so cute and well behaved, much better behaved than our own four kids who're always running around the neighborhood, getting into trouble and other assorted mischief. (Bobby, our youngest,

is on probation - help!) I don't
know why God sent them to us
but, well, they're ours and
we'll have to deal with it, even
though I admit on several
occasions I've thought of doing
what that woman did ten years
ago and driving all of them into
a lake in my car. I really
wouldn't do that but believe me
I've thought about it. Even
your mother in law seems so nice
and demure. I hope she lives to
be 100!

Anyway, I've got to scrub the
bathroom floor now then do the
laundry, so I'll sign off and
say, again, you have the best
family a man could possibly
want. You must be so proud.
Please keep up the good work,
and, again, good luck with that
evil Boehner.

Sincerely,

Christine Biggers

Modesto, TX

PS: I read in 'People' Magazine
that Boehner uses a sunlamp. Is
that true?

THE WHITE HOUSE

WASHINGTON

August 15, 2010

Dear Christine:

Thank you for your kind words about Michelle and the kids. They are extremely beautiful and as close to perfect as any parent could wish. (Michelle has to pick Malia up later at ballet practice and Sasha from piano lessons.) Times are tough for everybody these days, but please have hope and trust in our country.

Sincerely,

Barack Obama

Obama, Senators McCain and Schumer discuss what to do with a bowl of apples.

January 24, 2013

Dear Mr. President:

My name is Ron Kennedy. You don't know
me, but I'm a member of the younger
generation of Kennedy cousins which
includes Douglas, Michael, Mary, Rory,
Willie, Kara, Ted Kennedy, Jr. as well as
Caroline and Patrick, to name only a very
few.

Currently, I'm working at a Subway
Sandwich shop in Bethesda, MD. I enjoy my
job, and am in line for a promotion to
assistant manager, which I hope will
occur in the next few months.

At a recent Kennedy clan gathering at the
Kennedy clan compound in Hyannis Port, I
made a short speech about my uncle,
Senator Ted Kennedy, who as you know
passed away in 2009. I related how, when
waterskiing one summer with Uncle Ted, I
had taken a bad fall in the water. Back
in the tow-boat, I cried, and said I
never ever wanted to waterski again. But
then Uncle Ted took me aside and told me
I should absolutely never give up, and
that I should get back out on the water
and keep waterskiing until I get it
right.

Right after my speech, two of my cousins
(I forget which ones there's so many of
them) took me aside and told me how it
had reminded them of Uncle Ted, and also
of my two other uncles, John F. Kennedy
and Robert Kennedy, and wondered if I had
ever seriously considered entering
politics. My answer was that, despite my
famous last name, never once in my entire
life had I ever seriously considered
entering politics. For as long as I can
remember, I had always wanted to be
either a sports broadcaster or in the
catering business. When broadcasting
didn't happen, a Kennedy clan cousin
helped me get a job at a nearby Subway's,
and I discovered I thoroughly enjoyed it.

Almost six months have passed since my
speech, and even though I'm perfectly
happy being one of those rare breeds, an
"anonymous" Kennedy, I've come under
intense pressure from my cousins and the
extended Kennedy clan (which now includes
close to 12,000 people) to run for
elective office.

Several weeks ago, after consulting with
my other cousins, Sydney, Mark, Tim,
Anthony and Christopher, I decided I
should probably throw my hat into the
ring and make a run for the open
Massachusetts Senate seat recently
vacated by Senator Kerry.

As you know, Senator Kerry and Uncle Ted
were not only colleagues but also close
friends. (Even their last names are

similar.) No one will ever really
adequately fill Senator Kerry's shoes, or
certainly Uncle Ted's shoes, but
considering I'm under intense pressure to
fill his shoes by the entire Kennedy
clan, who if you recall supported you
strongly during your first as well as
second runs for president, it seems like
a golden opportunity I probably shouldn't
pass up.

Mr. President, before I take this
profound leap into the unpredictable and
sometimes distasteful morass of American
politics, I'd like to ask if I can count
on your support should I decide to run
for Senator Kerry's seat. If your answer
is 'yes', then I will immediately make an
announcement of my candidacy.

With your help, Sir, it is my intention
not only to help you, but to do whatever
is necessary to make America the great
country Uncle Ted, and the entire Kennedy
clan, had always hoped it could, and
should, be.

Sincerely,

Ron Kennedy

THE WHITE HOUSE

WASHINGTON

January 27, 2013

Dear Ron,

    Thanks for contacting me about your potential run for John Kerry's Senate seat. Massachusetts, the Bay State, has a proud liberal tradition which the entire Kennedy clan has played a huge and important role in maintaining.

    Please call the White House switchboard at 202-456-1414 and leave your telephone number and best time to call with my personal secretary, Katie Johnson. Either I or someone on my staff will then call you back so we can discuss your plans in more detail as well as coordinate a strategy.

    Good luck in whatever you should decide to do.

    Sincerely,

Barack Obama

2775 Midway Drive
Sebring, FL 33870

March 22, 2013

Dear President Obama,

My name is Lester Krinkle, and I'm a year-round resident of Sebring Florida.

I was out golfing last Saturday, when a giant sinkhole opened up as our foursome was standing on the seventh green. Luckily, we were able to escape at the last second and no one was hurt. But then, as we were driving our carts back to the clubhouse, I saw the exact same thing happen to another golfer, then once again in a trailer park just off Route 27 while we were heading home.

When I got back from the golf course I did some research on the internet (after telling my wife then taking a shower first), and discovered that sinkholes form when bedrock dissolves and holes or caves form in their place. After a BBQ dinner I did even more research, and discovered a definite pattern: sinkholes have been popping up almost everywhere, posing a threat to people, animals, golf courses -- probably our entire national security!

Mr. President, I realize you're probably busy as hell up there running things, but I definitely think we're in the midst of some kind of sinkhole epidemic that only some genius in Hollywood could dream up.

I don't know if they have anything like this up in the Washington D.C. area, but they sure have them down here in sunny Florida, and they're scary as hell!

Imagine this: it's a beautiful summer day, when all of a sudden the ground opens up and everyone in the USA is swallowed up by a monster sinkhole (or multiple giant sinkholes), where the only survivors are those survivalist groups you see on TV. Not only would many people be killed immediately, but our economy would be set back a hundred years as well, like what happened to Japan after that tragic tsunami 2 years ago.

For this reason, Sir, it's my firm belief you should now convene an emergency meeting of the Joint Chiefs of Staff, the CIA, the FBI, as well as the Department of Homeland Security plus all available members of Congress and get this dire problem seriously looked at.

President Obama -- sinkholes are for real. Please act before it's too late!

Sincerely,

L. Krinkle

November 22, 2011

Dear Pres. Obama:

You're probably going to find this letter a
little weird, but I'm writing it anyway 'cause I'm
a heap of trouble and I didn't know where else or
who else to turn to.

About two years ago I was working at a car wash
off I-45 near Huntsville (TX). The wages sucked,
but the work was steady and I had a ton of bills,
rent, and child support (total: $458.16 /week) to
pay and with all that I was barely making it. To
tell the truth, I was thinking of putting my
brother's 12-gauge in my mouth and ending it.

It was at that time a friend of mine, Digg
Cellars, told me I might consider enlisting in
the U.S. Army. I thought he was crazy, but, again,
I was in bad shape so I decided to check it out
anyway.

The enlistment officer I talked to explained the
whole thing, and it sounded so good I drove back
to the E.O. three days later and signed up.

Here's the truly sick part: the enlistment
officer never ever told me we were engaged in
two wars, in Iraq and Afghanistan, that I could
be sent to one (or even both) of those two places,
and that I could get my head and/or family
jewels blown off by an IED or enemy RPG.

Well, to make a long story real short, I'm typing
this on my i-Pad from Forward Operating Base
Salerno, about 45 klicks from Khost, in this
shallow trench where right now me and four

buddies are taking incoming rocket and mortar fire from a bunch of total a-holes called the Taliban!

Mr. President, I think I was lied to by that enlistment officer back in Texas, who deliberately withheld information from me and thus legally I don't think I should even be here. I should back in Texas with my three kids and ex, working at that car wash - anywhere but here.

I know you're busy with the struggling economy and Congress and everything, but is there any way, any way in hell, you could get a message to my platoon leader (1st Lieutenant Ed Glewicki) and tell him what I just old you? When I try to talk to him he tells me to "pull myself together" and "get my asshole in gear". (Sorry for the profanity but that's what he said). On the other hand, I have no doubt he'll listen to you, the Commander-in-Chief.

Thanks for your time, Sir.

Sincerely,

Del Czewiski

PFC 1st Class Del Czewiski

Khost, Afghanistan

(P.S. I voted for you even though my father told me he'd "break my neck" if I didn't vote for McCain.)

Michelle Obama holds a seance
with friends at the White House.

December 17, 2011

Dear Sir:

I know you're probably busier than a termite in a sawmill right now, but I decided to write you after sixteen frustrating years dealing with the Veterans Administration.

I was recently diagnosed with Parkinson's, which comes on top of a bad leg I picked up in Korea in 1952, a few years after I got home from the big one, WW 2, where I saw action in France and barely escaped fierce German machine gun fire on Omaha Beach. (Before you were even born.)

Long before D-Day and surviving the Great Depression by working in a coal mine in Kentucky, I lied about my age (I was only 12) and signed up with the Army way back in 1917 when Mr. Woodrow Wilson was President. I survived a mustard gas attack but only barely. I crawled back to my barracks, and was sent right back out where I witnessed the most unimaginable horrors any man has ever had to witness.

But even all that, Mr. President, was easy compared to dealing with the difficult people at the VA. You go in, sit for hours upon hours in the waiting room, and they barely even notice you or care you exist. And assuming you get to talk to a real person, you have to wait months and months before you can see a doctor, or even a nurse!

Frankly, it can take years off a man.

Is there anyway you or Mr. Panetta can call someone so I can be seen promptly and not have to wait sixteen whole years, again! In three more months I'll be 97, and with this Parkinson's I probably won't even be able to write a damn letter again, so it's either now or never.

Thanks so much for your attention to this matter.

Pvt. 1st Class Carlton Landers (US Army, Ret.)

Speck, North Dakota

BERKSHIRE HATHAWAY INC.

3555 Farnam Street

Suite 1440

Omaha, NE 68131

March 30, 2011

Dear Mr. President:

Thank you for your kind words last Saturday at The Kennedy Center Awards ceremony. As you know, being from Nebraska I generally avoid the spotlight. There was one benefit this time, however, which is that we were able to chat for a few minutes, and to share some of our concerns about the economy.

You asked during our private dinner later at the White House how I decide which companies to buy. Actually, you'd be surprised to know that my investing philosophy is quite simple, and can be summarized in a few bullet points:

- When considering whether or not to buy a company, contrary to popular belief I don't spend months or years poring over seemingly endless piles of company reports, a task I almost always find mind-numbingly tedious. Instead, I defer to my chauffeur of thirty years, Henry. If Henry gives a company the thumbs up, we purchase it.
- Knowing how much to pay for a company is equally critical. For this job, I usually consult my trusted gardener, Felipe. If Felipe frowns and says "Demasiado", I know the price is probably too high. If Felipe smiles broadly and says, "Si", I'll know we're about to pay the right amount.
- The stock market has always been a complete mystery to me. Knowing which stocks to pick is simple, however, if you've got a great dry cleaner -- like Mr. Ho. If Mr. Ho likes a stock I inquire about, he'll have my shirts ready promptly the following day. If he doesn't, he'll tell me to come back Tuesday afternoon.

- Sound management is the key to any company's ultimate success. If I'm considering hiring someone, I'll check with my mailman, Hank, first. He'll look at the fellow's resume, then give me either a thumb's up or a thumb's down. In fifty years he's never been wrong.

In general, I've found success in business to be a giant crapshoot in that there's absolutely no substitute for plain dumb luck. It also helps to spend a large part of your early professional life sitting alone in a wood-paneled basement in Omaha, studying probability theory.

Stay well, Mr. President, and let's talk again soon.

Sincerely,

Warren Buffett

WB/db

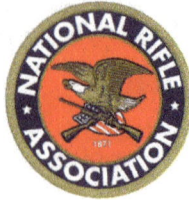

February 11, 2013

Dear President Obama:

Last Friday, along with many other Americans, I viewed your press conference on the subject of gun control in America. I am writing today to indicate my sincerest and most profound disagreement with your stance on this important, emotional matter.

As you well know, Sir, the inclusion of the 2nd Amendment in our hallowed Constitution was not placed there by the Founders as an afterthought, or by mistake. It was deliberately placed there to prevent exactly what you're trying to do today: to deprive America of its birthright -- guns.

Mr. President, America needs guns. America likes guns. I am not a fan of Hollywood in any way, which vilifies gun-owners while at the same time romanticizing gun-violence. Yet, the most successful movies, TV shows, video games, and even books feature guns in some prominent way. This proves that guns are extremely popular and that Americans like them -- a lot.

As I have said many times in the past, Sir, the NRA will not sleep for a single solitary second until each and every American, including children as young as four, have access to the same firepower carried by any character seen in any popular TV show or Hollywood movie. This includes, but is certainly not limited to, all pistols and rifles with magazines of any size and with any attachment(s), the MP/M9A1 57mm Bazooka and all other anti-tank weapons, rocket-propelled grenade launchers (7V2 thru RPG 32), AR-15's with up to 120-round magazines, the 40mm Beaufort (Russian) machine gun, the M61 Vulcan Auto cannon (Gatling gun), as well as any type of armored personnel carrier, minesweeper, and miniaturized low-yield (<5 KT) tactical nuclear weapon.

The only area where we agree is that these weapons should not be in the hands of any children younger than four years of age, New Yorkers, or any person currently in an institution for the <u>certifiably</u> criminally insane. (But not *after* their release.)

You said in your opening statement, Sir, that the Founding Fathers "could never have anticipated the carnage we're witnessing in our streets today…" due to guns. Mr. President, this is not gun violence we're seeing, but "people violence" -- sad, disturbed, lonely citizens killing and murdering other citizens using armaments of vast firepower with the potential for causing bucketfuls of bloody gut-ripping violence and assorted mayhem due to either mental illness, criminal intent, or some petty domestic argument.

Yet, in colonial times, is it not the fact, Sir, that these same sorts of emotions existed as well? Of course they did, so your left-wing liberal argument holds no water.

My organization, the National Rifle Association, will never reconsider even one syllable of our stance on guns until the American people, not the government, willingly agree to give up their only true God-given right: the right to bear arms.

Sincerely,

Wayne LaPierre, Ex VP

National Rifle Association

President Obama is caught
red-handed with a stolen apple by staff.

April 3, 2012

Dear Mr. President:

Amanda "Taffy" Huntington, the daughter of Dr. Winifred Smythe Huntington and Dr. Alexander Huntington of Cedarhurst, N.Y., is to be married Sunday evening to Alan Joel Finkelstein, a son of Dr. Avital Finkelstein and Dr. Marvin Finkelstein of Buffalo. The Reverend Trumbull Hyde-Smythe, the bride's maternal grandfather, is to officiate at the Noroton Presbyterian Church in Darien, Connecticut, with Rabbi Schlomo Rosenbaum taking part.

The bride, 24, is currently in her third year at Harvard Medical School. She graduated from Harvard University in three years, with a dual degree in art history and physics, Summa Cum Laude with highest honors. She spent the past summer travelling throughout Vietnam, China, and Inner Mongolia to prepare for a trip to India and Sudan after she graduates from medical school.

Her father is an endocrinologist and chairman of the Department of Medicine at The Massachusetts General Hospital in Boston. He is also a clinical associate professor of medicine at Harvard Medical School. Her mother is the P.T. Barnum Professor of Surgery at Harvard Medical School. Since 1977, she has been on the board of directors of Freeport-McMoRan, an international mining conglomerate and one of the world's leading producers of gold, copper, and molybdenum.

The groom, also 24, is in his second year at Harvard Medical School, after graduating from Harvard in one year with a degree in psychology and a minor in broadcasting. He was president of his undergraduate class, and spent the last summer travelling throughout Asia, the Middle East, Africa, and southern Europe to research a book on major league pitching greats, to be published in September by Knopf.

His father is the president and chief executive officer of Upstate Medical Solutions, Inc. of Buffalo, N.Y. The company was founded by the groom's great grandfather, Leo, and his great uncle, Mordechai. The groom's father is also chairman of WZZE, WZZA, and WXYZ, a group of terrestrial television stations he purchased in 1979. He is also the publisher and owner of "Teen Foto", an exploitation magazine focusing on underground teen culture in the Buffalo area. The groom's mother, also a doctor, is the chief operating officer of United Health Services, LLC, a medical collections company based in Darien, Connecticut. She is also the chief executive officer of Pay-Day Loans, Inc., a chain of pawnshops originally founded by her great grandfather, Levi, which operates in all fifty states and Canada.

Sincerely,

Jennifer Cosgrove

Secretary to Dr. Winifred Huntington

January 18, 2013

Dear President Obama:

My name is Kimberly Shrinker. I live in Hardin, Montana, where I am the assistant to the head librarian at Hardin Elementary. I recently finished reading both of your books, which I enjoyed very much.

In my spare time, I'm also a writer. As a writer yourself, and as President of the United States, I thought you could help me get a foothold in the writing profession. To date, I've written 349 short stories, 478 magazine articles, and 8 novels, each of which I've submitted to approximately 3,455 publishers. As of yet, I've received only rejection.

Mr. President, I think I'm a damned good writer, but I'm out here in Montana, (near Billings), a profoundly conservative, deeply religious state far from the publishing world, so it's hard to get started.

Below, is a sample of a new romantic novel I'm working on, tentatively entitled 'Helen's Morning', the full text of which I can send you when it's finished.

Helen awoke with a crushing, nearly blinding headache. Gazing across the bedroom at the shaft of early morning light pouring through the window, she wondered how she had made it back home the previous night. At almost the same moment, she saw the figure lying next to her in bed. It was the young man she had met at Kelsey's just before closing, only now he was naked. His long golden torso was hairless and well-toned, and aroused her immediately. Her success at finally landing such a perfect specimen, after so many nights, and now months, spent alone, made her chuckle. Suddenly, the man stirred, opened a pair of brilliant blue eyes, and looked at her small but shapely breasts lustfully...

Mr. President, a few people I've shown my work to say it reminds them of the 'Fifty Shades of Grey' book series, which as you know has sold millions of copies. The problem, again, is that I have no contacts.

If you could please pass along my excerpt to someone on your staff with connections in the publishing industry, I'd be eternally grateful. As you stated in your last speech, everyone needs a little help from time to time, and that's what I desperately need now.

Sincerely,

Kimberly Shrinker

18 Old Tree Lane

Hardin, Montana 59034

About the Author

Marc Berlin is a writer and filmmaker.
When not writing, he takes long walks in the cranberry bogs
near his home in eastern Massachusetts.

His website is at *www.marcberlin.net.*

www.ingramcontent.com/pod-product-compliance
Lightning Source LLC
Chambersburg PA
CBHW060744100426
42813CB00032B/3397/J